The Guy's Guide

to Surviving PREGNANCY,

CHILDBIRTH, and the

First Year of FATHERHOOD

# THE GUY'S GUIDE

*To Surviving* PREGNANCY, CHILDBIRTH, *and the* First Year *of* FATHERHOOD

## MICHAEL R. CRIDER

Da Capo
∞
LIFE
LONG

A Member of the Perseus Books Group

*Text Design by Jeff Williams*
Set in 11-point Adobe Garamond by the Perseus Books Group

Cataloging-in-Publication data for this book is available from the Library of Congress.

First Da Capo Press edition 2005
Originally published in 2002 as *Dada* by iUniverse.com.
ISBN 0-7382-1027-7

Published by Da Capo Press
A Member of the Perseus Books Group
http://www.dacapopress.com

Da Capo Press books are available at special discounts for bulk purchases in the U.S. by corporations, institutions, and other organizations. For more information, please contact the Special Markets Department at the Perseus Books Group, 11 Cambridge Center, Cambridge, MA 02142, or call (800) 255–1514 or (617) 252–5298, or email special.markets@perseusbooks.com.

1 2 3 4 5 6 7 8 9—09 08 07 06 05

*For Julie and the Little King . . .*

"By profession I am a soldier and take pride in that fact. But I am prouder—infinitely prouder—to be a father. A soldier destroys in order to build; the father only builds, never destroys. The one has the potentiality of death; the other embodies creation and life. And while the hordes of death are mighty, the battalions of life are mightier still. It is my hope that my son, when I am gone, will remember me not from the battle, but in the home repeating with him our simple daily prayer."

—Douglas MacArthur

# CONTENTS

## II. THE SECOND TRIMESTER
## (SAME AS THE FIRST)

## III. ROUNDING THIRD . . .

## IV. . . . AND BABY MAKES THREE

## V. WELCOME HOME

# FOREWORD

EVERY HIGH SCHOOL HAS ONE. The guy who could have moonlighted as a stand-up comic, always had a funny comeback, and tended not to take things too seriously. The guy you looked for in the halls after a miserable history exam. The guy who creatively named his cafeteria food. And the guy you couldn't picture as a family man. At my high school, that guy's name was Michael. As a member of the band, he took his drumming seriously. His Howie Mandel impersonation was dead-on. He was the guy who wouldn't think twice about mooning your mother. Seldom serious, he was the guy your parents worried you would one day choose to marry.

After high school, Michael did marry. He and his wife, Julie, moved away, and they were constantly asked by nagging relatives when they planned to have children. A gazillion years went by, and no kids. Anyone who knew Michael finally realized that kids might not be in his future.

Then, one day, my phone rang. "We're having a baby," Michael said. After congratulating him, I asked him how this happened. He attempted to give me the birds and the bees talk that parents give their preteens. He knew what I meant. Crazy. I still saw him as "Mike from high school," and he was about to become "Mike, the Dad." The kid was doomed.

Or so I thought. Throughout the next nine months, or ten, as Michael was quick to point out, he e-mailed friends and relatives pregnancy updates. He attached photos of Julie in maternity clothes, her baby shower, the nursery, etc.—he didn't miss a thing. Scared to death, he counted down the days to Julie's due date.

And then Michael found himself staring at a bluish-red miniature version of himself. This version of Michael was named Ryan, and as Michael snapped pictures, he immediately noticed that Ryan didn't look a thing like the blob on the ultrasound. Nope. Ryan was a real person. Michael was suddenly responsible for another life. Gulp.

That's right. The guy who wondered why the device that doctors used to listen to Ryan's heartbeat looked like a "glorified Mr. Microphone" was now a dad. The guy who responded with a hand gesture when cut off in traffic didn't care how long it took to drive Ryan home from the hospital. The guy who can easily bring a smile to your face is smiling at parenthood.

My phone rang last week. It was Michael, who now works from home to spend more time with Ryan. "I wrote a book about being a dad," he said. I smiled. As the mother of a five-month-old son, I know parenthood isn't easy, but it's the best gift in the world. And "Mike from high school" had figured that out. The shocks and joys of parenthood, told only like "Mike from high school" could.

Proud of ya, Mike.

—Deborah Honeycutt
WFMS Radio
Indianapolis

# INTRODUCTION

BEFORE I BEGIN, I guess I should make it clear that I am not a doctor. I don't even have a degree. In fact, I'll go you one better: I've flunked out of some of the finest collegiate institutions that central Indiana has to offer. So what leads me to believe that I have what it takes to write a parenting book? I have a baby, a computer with a word processing program, and a lot of spare time.

This certainly won't be a guide for everyone. This will be a father's guide. A guy's guide to fatherhood, if you will. Not that mothers or mothers-to-be aren't welcome here. They most certainly are welcome. In fact, the more, the merrier. However, ladies, be forewarned that a male's point of view on this subject is one that may be difficult for you to swallow. That being said, it's the only perspective that I have. I do not think myself qualified to give a female outlook on this topic. At last glance in the shower, I did not notice a vagina. (I did, however, notice a weird mole that I need to have examined. But I digress. . . . ) I'm a guy. Therefore, I'll give a guy's point of view on parenting. What I *won't* do is try to tell you new and/or expectant fathers what to do (incidentally, why the hell do they refer to those about to become parents as "expectant"? Believe me, you have *no* idea what to expect. The correct term would be more like "poor suckers who have no clue what you're in for"). I couldn't possibly begin to tell you what is right or wrong about the way you are raising your children.

I simply want to share my experiences and philosophies with you so that you may be able to take them and apply them to your life, either by saying "What a great idea!" *or* "Mother of God! What is this idiot thinking?" I intend to tell you about my experiences, both with my wife and my baby, with regular updates going through the first year of the baby's life. I'll tell you about the good times as well as the times when I was so tired and aggravated that I wanted to pinch my own head off rather than spend one more minute in this family. We'll laugh, we'll cry, we'll grab our collective crotch and break into song. It'll be a beautiful thing. Fair enough? OK, here we go. First, a little history. . . .

# PART ONE

# In the Beginning . . .

# The Pre-pregnancy
# Days of Wine and Roses

MY WIFE, JULIE, AND I have been together for over fourteen years now. We've been married for eleven years, but we lived together for the first few years of our relationship. I know a lot of people cringe at the thought of others "living in sin" or whatever, but I have to be honest; I would never, ever marry anyone without living with them first. You don't truly know a person until you spend a considerable amount of time under the same roof with them. You get to learn their idiosyncrasies, their true likes and dislikes. You learn the difference between their "date" mannerisms and their "real" mannerisms. You get to hear them fart for the first time. And more important, you find out whether or not the two of you are compatible. I cannot fathom marrying someone only to discover that I enjoyed their company a lot more when I was only around them a few hours at a time.

I have the same philosophy regarding premarital sex. How could you marry someone without first having sex with them? Would you buy a car without test driving it? Would you buy a house before seeing it? No. Hell no. What if the sex is bad? Imagine this scenario: It's your wedding day. You marry this perfect virgin bride. After a beautiful ceremony and a delightful reception, you retire to your honeymoon suite. Your nervous new wife steps into the bathroom to "freshen up," or pluck something, or whatever the hell it is they do in there. She emerges from the bathroom in her lingerie and approaches you. You're sitting at the edge of the bed anxiously awaiting your first sexual encounter, wondering if you should have considered a breath mint before now. You slowly remove her lingerie and "BAM!!!" you find out she doesn't have any genitals! (Hey, it could happen. It happened to my best friend . . . OK, not really.) You've just legally bound yourself to a woman who has the anatomy of a Barbie doll. And divorce is out of the question, because if you're the type of person who is so convinced that living together and having premarital sex is wrong, you most certainly are going to frown on divorce.

I know there will be those who will read that and say, "That's ridiculous. Living together and having premarital sex teaches couples to have the mind-set that commitment isn't important," and then they'll give the "Why buy the cow when you can get the milk for free?" analogy. Hey, that's fine. You have a right to your own opinion. But go write your own damn book and leave me alone. (Besides, that whole cow analogy doesn't apply to me; I'm lactose intolerant and not into animals.) I warned you in the beginning that this wouldn't be for everybody. It is my belief that living together and engaging in premarital sex can and often do prevent lifelong resentment in a relationship. Some may disagree with me, and that's fine. This is, after all, just my view. I could be wrong. I mean, I'm not, but theoretically, I suppose I could be.

So anyway, Julie and I were together for ten years before we had our first child. If I could hand out one piece of advice, it would be to wait as long as possible to have children. (Of course, if you bought this book, chances are you're already in the midst of the whole pregnancy thing. In which case, forget my advice. . . . ) Relationships need time to grow and to blossom. I'm so thankful for the years I had alone with my wife. We got to know each other, go on trips, and basically have fun for all those years without having the burden or responsibility of raising kids. I believe it was an essential element of our marriage, and it is one of the reasons that we'll have one of the few marriages that will last happily ever after.

Truth be told, we had all but decided not to have children at all. We were content in our current situation, and we both felt like our lives were complete. We could just keep on trucking along the way we had for all these years, and that would have been fine by us. Sure, we had wondered about who would take care of us in our "golden years." We wondered whom we could love unconditionally, bring up in a strict but loving environment, put through college, watch them marry the love of their life, give us grandchildren . . . and then watch them promptly stick our ass in some third-rate nursing home. We wondered all of these things, and this inevitably brought us to the conclusion that we would be antiparenthood. I mean, kids? Yeah, right. One big heartache after another. What's the point? No, let's go on about our lives having fun and doing whatever the hell we want. That's it. We made up our minds. No kids for us.

So that was our lifelong plan. But sometimes fate plays its fickle hand. . . .

# You're What?

JULIE HAD TOLD ME that she wanted to host one of those "lingerie parties" in our home. (For those of you unfamiliar with these "women only" parties, they're similar to Tupperware parties, only with dildos and crotchless panties.) Naturally, the thought of twenty women in my house playing with sex toys intrigued me, not to mention the fact that traditionally the hostess receives a discount on these items. So with the idea of cheap sex on my mind, I said yes. I think my exact words were, "Here's the checkbook. Have fun!"

The evening came and went and was, from what I understand, quite the success and a lot of fun. They had a good number of ladies show up at this gathering, had snacks that included pasta shaped like penises, and sold a lot of products that tasted like cinnamon and vibrated. Nothing kinky occurred, much to the dismay of the $12,000 hidden-camera system I installed the day before. Julie purchased a few items at the party, one of which was this "spermicidal lubricant." This lubricant was supposed to have a potent chemical that would kill my little tadpoles before they could invade my wife's egg. The description given to my wife was: "You can use this in place of any other form of birth control, including condoms, the pill, sponges, or diaphragms." So we thought, "Cool!" and immediately tried it out.

I have since read the fine print on this product, and of course there was no such birth control guarantee. The marketing department of the lubricant company should consider renaming this product with a more appropriate moniker, such as "Oops" or "Congratulations," because a few weeks later we found out that Julie was pregnant. (Incidentally, we found out she was pregnant on April 20, 1999—the same day as the now infamous slaughter at Columbine High School in Colorado. The news media would later refer to that day as "the darkest day of 1999." Great. . . . )

It started out as a normal day. (Remember that word: "normal." This word would take on a whole new life throughout the pregnancy and would continue to evolve after the baby was born.) My wife and I rode to work together, as we always did, because we worked across the street from each other. I got to the office ten minutes late, as was the standard at the time. I had my morning Coke, chit-chatted with fellow employees, and played on the Internet for six solid hours. Normal. But I must admit, I kept wondering when Julie would call to tell me that everything was fine and I could stop worrying.

*Call me, Julie,* I thought to myself.

*Come on.*

*Any time now.*

*Why won't the phone ring?*

*Hmm . . .*

Soon my mind was occupied with other things, such as work and which naked-celebrity Web site I could visit next. I was almost ready to go have lunch when the receptionist said, "Uh, Mike. Julie's on the phone. Sounds like she's crying . . ."

Shit.

Now, we had thought that she possibly might be pregnant. It *had* crossed our minds. I mean, her period was late, which was odd. But then, we had taken every store-bought pregnancy test known to the Western Hemisphere. I went out to the drugstore, spent an obscene amount of cash on six different kinds of these tests, and after she'd peed on them all saw no conclusive evidence that she was pregnant. Five of the six tests were negative. Only one of the tests had a suspicious little line on it. See, if the test was positive, there would be a "+." If the results were negative, a "–" would appear. This particular test had kind of a half-assed plus sign. Again, nothing absolute. Just enough to make us decide that she needed to have a blood test done at the doctor's office. So she had the test and was supposed to get the results on this particular day. OK, I guess that pretty much brings us up to speed. So . . . Where was I? Oh, yeah.

Shit.

I took a deep breath and said, "Hey." Julie's weepy reply (and I'll *never* forget this as long as the beer doesn't kill all my brain cells) was, "Mike . . . *sniff* . . . the damn thing was positive!" I said, . . . well, I don't exactly know what I said. But it was probably something along the lines of "It'll be OK. I love you. I'll be right there." At least I hope that's what I said. Hell, I might have said something resembling "I like eggs." I have no idea. I was in complete shock.

Shock or not, I knew I had to try to rescue my damsel in distress. To do so, I attempted to leap up from my desk and dash to her side. What I discovered at this point was that I couldn't move. I simply could not move. My entire body just stayed put, no matter how hard I negotiated with it to move. This was like one of those dreams where you try to run but your legs are too heavy. Or like when you try to punch someone in a typical nightmare and discover that no matter how hard you swing, you just barely tap their shoulder. Eventually, I was able to give myself a pep talk, which consisted of "Get up, dumbass!" Then, once I had my bearings, I bolted across the street to her office so fast that even Flo-Jo would have been proud, had she not been dead at the time. I found my wife standing on the steps of her office building, her eyes red and puffy from crying, looking like someone who had just been informed that she had a person growing inside of her, which of course, is exactly what she was. She looked shocked, frightened, and confused. But at that moment, she never looked more beautiful. I still can't really explain it. But she was now more than just my wife, more than just the woman I had known since we were in our teens. She was now going to be the mother of my child, and I was in awe. Not only in awe of the situation that we now found ourselves in; I was in awe of *her*.

I had such conflicting emotions at this particular moment. Remember, this was something we'd been avoiding for ten years. We'd had "close calls" where we thought she was pregnant. And each time, when we eventually found out that she was not pregnant, we were ecstatic. We were of the opinion that "Baby = Bad. No Baby = Good." We thought of parenthood as lost freedom, a prison sentence of sorts, in which you have a minimum of eighteen years without a chance of parole. But on the other hand, we had been happily married for such a long time that having a baby seemed like the next logical step. And I also knew that any baby that exited my wife's body would be a beautiful one. So how was I supposed to feel? Elated? Pissed? Terrified? Shocked? A little hungry? (Remember, I hadn't had lunch yet.) I felt all these things at once, each emotion fighting for the dominant position. It was all so confusing. After years of thinking that being a parent was a fate worse than death, now I'm supposed to be *happy* about this? My head was swimming, and I couldn't believe what I was hearing. It still seemed all too surreal. And so it will likely be for you when you first hear the words, "I'm pregnant." (Or in my case, "The damn thing was positive!") The entire world around you will just stop, and even if you've been *trying* to get her pregnant for ten years, you'll realize a few things:

1. Holy Lord, I'm going to be a daddy! Me? I'm not an adult yet! I still have my comic books and KISS dolls, for God's sake . . .
2. I have to get the baby on my health insurance program.
3. We've been drinking every weekend like Kennedys at a wedding reception. Is our baby going to be OK?
4. I have to call my mommy.

All of this goes through your mind in the first thirty seconds after you find out you're going to be a father. Then after those thoughts, you catch yourself and say, "Wait a minute. I guess I should hug her and find out if she's OK with this." That's when you discover that she's experiencing the same emotions and the same confusing thoughts that you are, only she's bawling uncontrollably due to the fact that her hormones are freaking out like Robert Downey Jr. at a rave. So that's when you kick into "protective mode" and console her. I must have said, "It'll be OK" about seventy-eight times that day.

But the truth is, you don't *know* if everything's going to be OK. There is so much that could go wrong during a pregnancy. How do you know everything will be OK? You don't. You can't possibly know. But you can't say to your scared, newly pregnant wife, "Sit still! Stop crying or you might accidentally kill the baby! For the love of John Tesh, don't do *anything* for the next nine months!!"

So to ease your fears, you reach for one of those books with titles like *What to Expect When You're Expecting* or *So You've Decided to Screw Up Your Life by Having Kids*, but they only make matters worse. The authors of these books tell you about every bad pregnancy scenario known to man. As a result, every time my wife sneezed or coughed I was ready to leap down and catch any premature baby that might shoot out of her. But anyway, back to what I was saying . . .

We immediately phoned everyone we'd ever met to tell them the news. Everyone was excited, especially our parents. My mother had been riding us for years to have a baby. She wanted so badly to join the "Grandparents Club" and she was finally getting her wish. Other people's reactions were mixed. Most everyone we spoke with said they were happy for us. While my parents were overwhelmed with excitement, Julie's parents were shocked. Of course they were happy for us, though frankly it is my belief that they felt they were too young to be grandparents. My best friend laughed. A lot. My boss was mostly concerned about whether or not I'd be missing a lot of work because of this. But the general consensus was that this was a good thing, and everyone was happy for us. My grandmother even told me she was proud of me. For what, I'm not exactly sure. I mean, screwing your wife is to be expected; it's natural. It's not an accomplishment like splitting the atom. But you take any encouraging words you can get, right? After we told everyone, Julie and I sat down together on the couch. My little incubator smiled at me with one single tear welling up in her eye, and we just hugged each other for a very, very long time.

As I said, the father-to-be protective instinct sets in shortly after the reality of the situation has taken hold. You will almost immediately want to guard your unborn child and your wife. I walked around for weeks with one arm covering my wife's belly. What exactly I was protecting it from, I'm not sure. Perhaps falling rocks? Stray bullets? SCUD missiles? I didn't know, but I was sure as hell not going to let anything happen to my family. No sir. Not on my watch. In retrospect, I needed to relax. I needed . . . a drink.

# Pregnancy:
# A Sobering Experience?

**AS A SUPPORTIVE HUSBAND** and hands-on father, guess what you will quit doing? That's right. You'll swear off things like alcohol, cigarettes, fatty foods, and heroin, or whatever you're into. You'll spout off things like, "I'm going to give up drinking. If my wife has to quit drinking and start eating right, I will too." This makes sense at the time you espouse it, and it is appreciated by your wife. She sees that you are taking an active role in the pregnancy and that you're being responsible. And you're proud of yourself.

You're thinking, "I'm a great husband. Good for me. I rock. If I had one of those shirts that said '#1 Dad' I'd wear it with pride right now." This feeling will last until the first beer commercial you see on TV. At that time, you will start rationalizing your beer drinking to your wife and to yourself. "You know, it's really not doing the baby any harm for ME to have a beer or two. Or six. Right? And the Pepsi? Well, there's already a twelve-pack in the fridge. And we don't want that to go to waste, either. Right? Honey? Honey?" At this point, you'll notice a look of disappointment in the eyes of your wife, who just ten minutes ago was bragging on your newly found self-discipline to her friend over the phone. She will marvel over the fact that it took you less than the full length of a thirty-second commercial to go from "Brand New Man" to "Same Old Shithead." Now, this is a pivotal point. You have two options here: You can get all defensive about the reaction you're receiving from her, and go on some ill-advised rant like, "Well, you're the one who went and got yourself pregnant! Why should I have to suffer, too?" but this will only buy you a two-night stay at the luxurious "Hotel Couch." Or you could just hang your head in shame, admit that you are a weak and lowly slimeball, and enjoy your beer in the next room.

So the bottom line is this: When it comes to the whole self-discipline thing, don't even try it. Your heart is in the right place, but your willpower is crap. The sooner you deal with it, the sooner you can move on to other important things, like "Where would be a good place to hide this pack of cigarettes so that the psycho-hormonal woman won't find them?"

# Decisions, Decisions

## NOW WHAT?

I'll tell you "now what." Now you wait. And wait. And wait. For us fathers, pregnancy is one long period of waiting. For the mothers, the waiting is accompanied by weight gain and increasing discomfort, but remember, this isn't a book about *their* experience, it's about ours!

Groucho Marx once said, "Time flies like an arrow. Fruit flies like a banana." I can appreciate what he was saying about your life quickly passing before your eyes, but the laws of time and space do not apply when it comes to pregnancy. The waiting during this period is maddening. We thought the little tyke would never get here. Here's a little-known fact: The average human gestational period is approximately six years. Or at least that's how it seems, although it is actually only forty weeks (which, your wife will remind you as though you owe her *extra,* is actually ten long months, not the nine they try to pass off to you in sex ed! Oh, and take it from me, "only" isn't a word you should use to precede "forty weeks" in her presence). You need something to occupy your mind during this time. So you decide to start planning things. But at this point it's still too early to choose your route to the maternity ward. And you can't exactly plan for what the baby will wear home from the hospital. I mean, she just discovered that she is with child. You have months and months to make these decisions. So you start the "name game."

We immediately went out and got books full of baby names. One book we bought included 20,000 baby names with the meaning and origin of each name! 20,000 names! How could we possibly be expected to narrow that list down to one name? It took us a week to name our kitten, for Pete's sake. (Just a quick side note: We named the kitten Oliver. I knew you were wondering. . . . ) Now we had to try to name a *person*? This seemed like way too much pressure.

Julie and I immediately agreed on . . . nothing. In theory, this ought to have been easier. But we found that we could not agree on a name at all. I couldn't believe we weren't able to come to some sort of agreement on this. Here I'd been convinced that we thought so much alike, but I was greatly mistaken. It is my firm belief, and I think I'm being fair here, that every name that came out of my wife's mouth was dumber than the last. And she thought the names I suggested were so contemptible that she almost left me over them.

If we were going to have a boy, I wanted to name him something slightly more traditional than what we were finding to be all the rage in the late 1990s, such as Taylor, Zack, Austin, Jacob, Cameron, Jordan, Justin, Blake, Cody, and so on. All of these names were fine in and of themselves, but I figured if he was in school and the teacher said, "Taylor, could you come to my desk, please?" seven little boys *and* four girls would have surrounded the teacher. "Did you mean me? I thought you meant me. You said 'Taylor' so I naturally assumed you meant me. . . ." It would be anarchy. So I personally preferred a name that was more conventional, but not too stuffy.

Julie, on the other hand, was leaning more toward the unique names ("unique" being Latin for "ridiculous"). I eventually had to tell her that if I have to look a name up to figure out how to spell it, then she could forget that particular name. This kid is going to find life to be challenging enough. He shouldn't have to strain to remember how to spell his own God-awful, whacked-out name.

One thing we actually agreed on was that we didn't want a name that was too "old fashioned." We weren't real hip on the idea of naming our kid something like Edith, Walter, Harlan, Myrtle, Prudence, or George. Again, not that there's anything wrong with these names, so please don't send me any hate e-mails over this. (Oh, OK, go ahead. My e-mail address is mstmrc@yahoo.com.) We just needed to find some sort of middle ground where we would agree to meet on this subject. Finally, after months of discussions and threats of lawsuits, we compromised and decided on our first-born's name. If we had a girl, she would be Abby. If we had a boy, he would be Ryan. We shook on it and made it an official deal.

Now that the naming task was done, we were ready for parenthood, and we just had to wait for the baby to arrive. Right? Um . . . no. Little did I know that we had only begun to scratch the surface on what would be a long and arduous process of decision-making.

There are literally thousands of other things to decide on.

What kind of bed will the baby have?
Should the baby be breast-fed or bottle-fed?
What color should we paint the baby's room?

Should we find out the sex of the baby during the ultrasound exam so that we can actually shop for some of this stuff?

Will we go with a natural childbirth?

Cloth diapers or disposable?

What about discipline?

Will we paddle or just do "time outs," like most of our friends were doing?

Are pacifiers a good thing or a tool of the devil?

Am I going to survive this whole ordeal?

These are just a few of the questions you'll ask yourself. Then after you've finally decided what you want, you'll realize that your wife has already made these decisions, and you've wasted your time even thinking about it at all.

That's when you realize that your role in the decision-making process is to just agree with everything your wife says and say, "OK." Now is not the time to argue with her. She's hormonal, gassy, and flat-out nuts. Simply nod politely, say "OK," whip out your credit card, place it in her swollen fingers, and slither off somewhere to have that beer that you're still feeling so guilty about enjoying.

# Eating for Three

GET USED TO IT: You're going to feel quite useless through most of your wife's pregnancy, certainly the first trimester. There's just not much you can do. There wasn't much I could do for Julie other than be supportive, which amounted to holding her hair when she barfed. I was already used to doing this from our partying days, so I was fairly well schooled in this craft (by the way, you just haven't lived until you've seen corn fly out of your wife's nose from the vegetable soup she had earlier that day). Luckily, Julie didn't have real bad bouts with morning sickness. She only got sick twice. The first time was the vegetable soup incident. The second was on a plane en route to Florida. She lost her crackers in the motion sickness bag given to us upon boarding the plane. Then she gave it to me to dispose of. "What the hell am I supposed to do with this?" I asked. "I don't know," she said. "Give it to the flight attendant. I don't care. Just get it out of my sight before I kill you." (Hormones. Wow . . . ) So when the flight attendant finally strolled by, I had to get her attention and say, "Pardon me. Could I get a ginger ale and a water? Oh, and here's a little something for your trouble."

But it's no wonder that women launch a liquid rainbow out of their mouth during this period, given some of the bizarre foods they ingest. Some women crave odd things during pregnancy, such as the old stereotypical pickles and ice cream. But be forewarned: Some mothers-to-be even eat glass and rocks at this time! Seriously! Glass and rocks! What is this all about? Are they having a baby or culturing a pearl?

In retrospect, I guess I got off light. Julie only craved normal foods. (There's that "normal" word again; see how its meaning is changing already?) Julie only wanted cereal for the first couple of months, which is relatively tame compared to the rock-and-glass chewers out there. During her pregnancy, my wife consumed enough Cheerios to fill a swimming pool. General Mills should be cosponsoring this book; God knows we inflated their revenue for second quarter of the 1999 fiscal year.

If Hollywood and books have taught us anything, it's that women will eat a lot of weird stuff during pregnancy. That's a given. What they *don't* tell you about is a little something called "sympathy pregnancy weight." This is a phenomenon that occurs around the time your partner and mother-to-be is two months pregnant. Since you aren't able to do the things you used to do with your partner, like sky-diving or slam-dancing at a Pantera concert, you share a new hobby with her: eating. I fell into the trap in which a lot of fathers-to-be fall: In order to be supportive of my pregnant wife's newly found appetite, I would not only buy the food she craved, I would join her in the indulgence of the craved items. The only problem is that she was eating for two and getting that cute little hard belly, and I was just getting to be a fat bastard. I realized that the worst part of this was that after she had the baby, she'd lose the pounds and I'd have gained so much weight that I'd have to wash myself with a rag on a stick to reach all the back fat.

Right about the time my wife had gained five pounds (and I'd gained ten), the fear of my own mortality came crashing in. I know what you're thinking: "That'll never happen to me. I can eat an entire rack of beef and not gain weight. I'm healthy, and I won't worry about such trivial things as death or obesity." Right. Whatever you say, Tubby. What will happen is this: You'll stare at the last bite of what was your seventh piece of pizza and suddenly it will dawn on you—"I'm going to die. I'm going to have a massive stroke, and I'm going to assume room temperature. My child will never know who I was. My family will end up living on the streets with no food or clothing! I need to quit eating so shittily (if that's a word) and go work out immediately!" So you'll decide to do a push-up or two, something will go "pop" in your shoulder, and you'll call it quits. I mean, no sense in overexerting yourself on the first day, right? The next day, you'll go running. Or at least you'll think about it. Then you'll think of reasons not to.

"Hmm . . . it looks like it might rain two counties over. Better not tempt fate. You just never know when a rainstorm might creep up on you. Then if I get rained on, I might get pneumonia and die. And that just seems counterproductive. Maybe I'll just try other forms of exercise for the moment." So instead of running, perhaps you'll do more push-ups. Uh-oh. Now your arms hurt from yesterday's push-up incident. Well, let's just wait for a day or two. At least until the old arms heal and the threat of severe weather passes. . . .

After a week or so, you'll have resumed your old eating habits and the most exercise you get will be trying to open a new bag of chips, and you'll get winded doing it. Then you'll come to the realization that you're probably not going to die today, and if you just relax, everything will be fine. But you'll want to increase your life insurance policy just in case.

# What's Up, Doc?

BEING THE SUPPORTIVE HUSBAND and hands-on father that you are, you will tell your wife early on that you will attend as many of her doctor appointments as you can. Little do you realize that this will eat up all the spare time you have.

I don't think *doctors* spend as much time in a doctor's office as we did when my wife was pregnant. First, you visit the doctor once a month. Then it becomes twice a month. By the end of the pregnancy, you're going anywhere between once a week to once a day! And these aren't exactly pleasant experiences. By God, you just haven't lived until you've seen a doctor get elbow-deep into your wife's birth canal for the first time. And you can tell by the look on your wife's face that she'd much rather be doing something more pleasant, such as smacking her own shins with a ball-peen hammer. This procedure that the doctor is performing (which is known in the medical profession as "the checking of the goodies") appears painful, and from what I understand, it is. I'm not sure what the doctor was checking for; perhaps checking to make sure my wife actually has a uterus and is, therefore, indeed pregnant. I mean, it's not like you can peek up there and see a baby hanging out, twiddling its newly formed thumbs. So I'm not sure what the point of this whole thing is. Perhaps that's why I'm not a licensed physician.

When the doctor was finished, she proclaimed, "Everything looks great." What's the reply here? "Thank you for the compliment on my wife's vagina. I was hoping you'd notice?" Whatever. "Looks great" is a good thing, so we just let it be.

Then comes the most nerve-racking part of the entire day. The doctor takes what is essentially a glorified Mr. Microphone and places it on your wife's stomach. I half expected to hear the baby say, "Hey good lookin'. We'll be back to pick you up later!" The job of this microphone is to pick up the sound of your baby's heart. But be fore-warned: It takes a while to pick up the heartbeat. Just know that much going into it. No one told me this, unless they did and I just wasn't listening, which is entirely possible. There was one hot nurse in the building that I kept stealing glances at, and I may have missed half the conversation. Anyway, I didn't know what to expect. I figured that the doctor would just plop that little thingamajig down on my wife's tummy and we'd immediately hear the thumping of a heart. But it takes a while. In fact, it seemed as though it took an eternity. That's when you start to worry that something might be wrong, even though the doctor has now said, "I told you at least three times that it might take a while to find the heartbeat." (Fine, so I definitely wasn't listening. I was checking out the little blonde nurse, OK?) Then suddenly, you hear a magic little sound. It's a sound that can only be described as "fast."

The baby's heart rate at the time was 154 beats per minute. Think about how fast that is! I mean that's faster than . . . well, faster than something going 153 beats per minute. (Sorry, I drew a blank.) It's amazing how fast the baby's little ticker was ticking. At first I was concerned that 154 beats per minute was too fast, but the doctor assured me that this was normal. (Psst . . . there's that word again: "normal." See how it's starting to take on a different meaning?) When I heard the baby's heart, I was afflicted with a feeling of cramping in my face, and it took a moment for me to realize where that feeling was coming from. I was smiling a big, goofy smile that can only come when you first hear your baby's heart beating. The very first time you hear the sound of your baby's heartbeat, overwhelming joy takes over your psyche. I mean, for perhaps the first time, this whole thing starts to make sense: There's a baby in there! A living being is forming in your wife's womb! Wow! That was really the first time that everything just sort of clicked for me. It was then that I truly realized that we weren't just going through this whole mess for no good reason. We were really going to be parents! Parents of a child who had, from what I could tell, a very strong heartbeat. Once again, Dr. Jellyfinger gives you a nod and a smile.

Positive feedback from your wife's doctor is exactly what you want to hear. You want to know that everything is OK, that your wife is OK, that the baby is OK, and that you are going to be OK. It's truly amazing how when two little letters like "O" and "K" are placed side by side, they have the power to soothe your nerves. So even though you've just witnessed a really disturbing examination, you can now take solace in the fact that the doctor is smiling and giving you encouraging words. Certain things you *wouldn't* want the doctor to say might include:

1. Dear God! What the hell is that?
2. Get me a bucket, I'm going to be sick . . .
3. Oops.
4. Everything looks entirely abnormal. You're a freak. Please leave.
5. What happened to my wristwatch?
6. Would you ask your husband to stop drooling over my nursing staff?
7. Seriously, what the hell is that?

After you get the doctor's seal of approval and everything looks good, you can look forward to the next visit, which features more crotch probing and more words of encouragement. And if you're disappointed that the appointment is over, don't despair. You have three to four hundred more of these lovely visits to go. Yippee! Are you sorry yet that you've decided to be supportive and hands-on? You're not, are you? Good man. Just what I wanted to hear. Read on, friend. . . .

# PART TWO

# The Second Trimester
# (Same as the First)

# Everything You Won't Need
# but You'll Buy Anyway

CONGRATULATIONS! You've made it through the first trimester. While the first three months are the most critical and sometimes most harrowing times during your bride's pregnancy, the second trimester is, on average, a little more relaxed. There seems to be less of a chance that things will go awry, your wife has a cute little pooch that keeps growing by the day (which probably makes her happier because now it's clear she's pregnant and not just getting fat), strangers are starting to notice and are wanting to touch your wife's belly, and you get to start picking out cool things like strollers.

Yes, I said strollers. It's incredible how your priorities change. For me, shopping for strollers took the place of looking for things like electronics or guitars. It soon became an obsession. I wanted the best stroller my grandmother's money could buy. (Hey, she offered. . . . )

They can do such amazing things with strollers. You just wouldn't believe it. We picked out the Cadillac of strollers. There were more cup holders, pockets, compartments, and buttons on this thing than there were on my first two cars combined. Of course, it cost more than the gross national product of Lithuania. But nothing is too good for *my* baby, right? Particularly when I'm spending someone else's money.

While strollers are an important item, there are literally thousands of other things you'll be convinced that you need for this child. When you walk into one of these stores like Babies "R" Us, Baby Warehouse, or Babies-a-Million, your senses are inundated with products you never even knew existed. And instead of rationally remembering that there is a whole industry dedicated to preying on you at this vulnerable time, you just feel vulnerable. Now you find yourself thinking, "If I don't have every single item in this store, especially all the safety stuff, I will be a bad parent and the state will take away my kid." And it's not even your fault that you feel that way. My God, look what the boxes for these products have printed on them. "Electric bottle warmer: A MUST for any new baby." A MUST? Really? Is this some kind of weird law that I wasn't informed of? They put all of these things in the stores to confuse you into buying this useless crap. Just as an example, here's an *abbreviated* list of things you'll feel compelled to buy. Sure, some of these things are necessary for your newborn, but can you tell which are not? For your firstborn son or daughter, all these things *sound* essential, don't they? Those marketers, they've got you by the short and curlies now.

| | |
|---|---|
| stroller | bottle washer |
| jogging stroller | bottle dryer |
| car seat | bibs |
| highchair | burp cloth |
| electrical outlet covers | crib |
| bottles | cradle |
| nipples | mattress |
| pacifiers | bedding |
| bottle warmers | bumpers |
| cupboard and drawer latches | changing table |
| onesies | portable crib |
| shirts | baby backpack |

| | |
|---|---|
| sweaters | infant swing |
| pants | bouncy seat |
| hats | bath seat |
| mittens | baby monitor |
| socks | night light |
| shoes | mobile |
| splat mats | wind-up music boxes |
| sippy cups | teething rings |
| diapers | support pillows |
| wipes | Barney books |
| diaper genie | activity gym |
| diaper bag | |

and toys that they'll never play with but will puke on at least twice. Did I miss anything? Probably.

Do you know what you *really* need for your newborn? Diapers, clothes, blankets, and a pair of breasts to suck on. That's it! The rest are just extras. I mean, electrical outlet covers? What kind of three-week-old is manhandling electronic devices at this stage? Don't let them dupe you into spending two-thirds of your annual salary on this crap. Just buy the absolute necessities. The rest will come later—and with luck, much of it in gift form! Trust me, you'll get plenty of chances to spend money on your little sperm-in-Nikes. For now, do as God intended. Have your parents buy all this useless junk for you. They'll be more than happy to spoil their new grandchild.

Now comes setting up the baby's room. You know, the baby's room? No? Oh, you're not familiar with this room? Well, perhaps you'll recognize it by what it's currently known as: Your music room. It's the extra room that you proclaimed as your own when you moved into your house. It's the room that you used to escape to when your wife was watching some bullshit movie on the Lifetime network, usually starring Judith Light from TV's *Who's the Boss?* that deals with how horrible men are. Now that room, your sanctuary, is going to be covered top to bottom in fluffy bunnies and baby accessories. But that's fine, because you are a supportive husband and a hands-on father. Remember? So take down the Budweiser mirror and the poster of the big-tittied model wearing a "Got Milk?" T-shirt that you thought was so damn funny when you were shopping stoned at Spencer Gifts. You're being evicted. This may be the first time you realize that not only is the baby consuming all of your thoughts and conversations, but it's also taking over your house! And the weirdest part is, *the baby isn't even here yet!*

Arriving at a theme for your child's bedroom is more stressful than you might imagine. You have to consider quite a few things:

What color should the walls be?

Should we go with a unisex theme, or should we wait to decorate until we find out the sex of the baby at the ultrasound? I mean, if we don't find out the sex and go with something too girlie and we have a boy, will he turn out gay?

Maybe we should wait for the ultrasound.

But then again, what if the ultrasound is wrong?

Will our daughter grow up to be a tattooed truck driver if we go with the border with the miniature cars on it because the ultrasound monitor had a speck of dust on it which resembled a penis, so we thought we were having a boy?

Yeah, let's wait for the ultrasound.

And should we put those little glow-in-the-dark stars up on the ceiling, so the baby thinks it's out on a camping excursion in the middle of the wilderness somewhere?

Can we wait until the ultrasound?

And how bad will this motif get on our nerves after staring at it for hours on end while trying to calm a screaming newborn at 3:00 a.m.?

All valid points (well, mostly). So we decided to hold off on decorating until after we went in for the ultrasound.

# Does This Thing Get HBO?

I, LIKE MOST OTHER MEN, LOVE GADGETS. I love electronic devices. I love anything that beeps, shows pictures, or surrounds me with loud sounds. My mouth waters at the thought of things with buttons and knobs and products that deal with words like "frequency," "hertz," and "ohms." I love going to electronics stores to look at televisions, radios, and other kinds of expensive stuff that my wife rarely allows me to buy. So my penchant for these doohickeys made me truly look forward to the ultrasound. The prospect of actually getting to play with this toy, as well as seeing a picture of my baby on television for the very first time, captivated me.

For those who are unfamiliar with the ultrasound, it is a diagnostic tool that has become very useful in obstetrics. The ultrasound devices in current use are known as real-time scanners, which produce a continuous picture of the moving fetus on a monitor screen. Very-high-frequency sound waves of 3.5 to 7.0 megahertz (i.e., 3.5 to 7 million cycles per second) are generally used for this purpose. They are emitted from a transducer, which is placed on top of the mother's abdomen and is moved about in order for you, the viewing audience, to get a look at the baby and/or any particular content of the uterus. (In layman's terms, they rub what looks like a pricing gun over your wife's belly until you get a picture so grainy you are too embarrassed to admit that, to you, what you're looking at could either be a baby or a police sketch artist's depiction of the Pillsbury Doughboy being accidentally heated up in a microwave.) You'd think that with this remarkable technology we have today, they could make an ultrasound image that would look like digital cable. But what do I know?

So the technician starts the process by squirting this clear, jelly-looking goo onto your wife's stomach (in my case, eerily similar to the clear, jelly-looking goo that promised to keep us out of this situation in the first place), then places the transducer on top of the goo. Then she moves it around until you start to see, for the very first time . . . the baby.

This is an amazing moment. Remember when you heard the heartbeat for the first time? Remember how thrilled you were and how you had to pry the smile off your face when you heard that sound? Well brother, that ain't nothin'! Wait until you actually *see* this little person on the monitor for the very first time. You'd never guess that a grainy black-and-white picture could affect you like this. I've been struggling to find ways to describe this feeling. Ways to tell you what to expect. How you'll feel. What you'll be thinking. How hard you'll be gripping your wife's hand in sheer excitement and joy. But I can't. This is something you'll have to experience on your own. I will promise you this: These feelings you'll be having, as wonderful as they are, will be second only to the first time you get to kiss your baby. But let's not get ahead of ourselves. Let's get back to the ultrasound.

I do believe that it's a universal phenomenon that you'll be anxious at this point, because the ultrasound will ultimately show if everything is fine with the baby, or if there is some sort of deformity. A little jelly goo and an electronic pricing wand stand between you and a sigh of relief. I personally breathed *two* sighs of relief after hearing that

A. everything was fine with our baby;

B. there was indeed only *one* baby in there (thank you, God).

If you're like me, it'll be at this point that you'll relax and start counting fingers, toes, looking at the ribs, the spine, the size and shape of the head . . . all kinds of cool stuff, even if you really have no idea what you're looking at! Then comes the big question from the technician: "Do you want to know the sex of the baby?"

For us, this was a no-brainer. We definitely wanted to know if we were having a boy or a girl. I have friends who didn't want to know the sex of the baby. They said they wanted to be "surprised." Well, I've got news for you. You're going to be dealing with plenty of surprises during the first year of parenthood. I don't think one little peek at the baby's plumbing is going to ruin the experience on the whole for you. Besides, it's a surprise no matter when you find out.

So we agreed that we wanted to know what we were having. As I said earlier, we had room-decorating issues that needed to be resolved ASAP. Plus, it is my belief that if God didn't want us to know the sex of the baby, he wouldn't have created the ultrasound machine in the first place (that must have been sometime during the eighth day, perhaps after he grabbed a quick nosh and a little nap).

After we answered the technician with a resounding, "Yes! We absolutely want to know the sex of the baby!" she moved the cursor on the monitor screen over to what doctors refer to as "the crotch." There, in all its glory, was . . . a *penis!* Even I could tell. The stem was on the apple! We were going to have a boy! "Ryan" was on the way. This was an exciting, life-defining moment.

Then the technician said something I found a little odd. She looked at the screen, pointed to my unborn son's lower torso and said, "Wow, what a penis!" Now, I wasn't sure how to feel about this. I mean obviously there is a certain amount of pride in hearing this from a technician who must see twenty unborn penises a day. Ryan was apparently advanced in the penile department, which made me kind of want to say, "Atta boy!" At the same time, what kind of person makes a big dick comment about an unborn child? And was she commenting on it because it was freakishly huge? Of course, for my son's sake I naturally hope he has satisfactory (if not slightly above average) sized genitals. But now she had me thinking that this penis might be circusworthy, like my kid would end up in a traveling freak show or something: "Come see the boy with the penis so large, it actually has an elbow!" But then I figured I was just nervous. Unsure of the protocol, I decided not to ask how Ryan's privates compared.

After finishing the ultrasound and getting the "Everything's OK" from the technician, she gave us a videotape of the ultrasound session, and handed us printouts of our baby's first photo shoot. (Complete with a shot of his penis, with an arrow pointing to it; again, I'm feeling a little awkward about this obsession she has with my son's genitalia . . . ) But I was so overwhelmed with excitement by the photos, I almost asked if they offered wallet-sized versions of them. Since it was obviously too early to have a family portrait done, I wanted to show off my kid in some way. Honestly, had my wife allowed me to do so, I would have had all of the ultrasound photos blown up to 8 by 10, professionally framed and displayed throughout the house. (Except for the penis shot of course; that's just plain wrong, and I'm quite sure it would be illegal in this state. And frankly, who wants to look at an 8 by 10, grainy, black-and-white picture of a penis, anyway?) I just wanted to show the whole world what I had made.

We left the office with a sense of relief that the baby was seemingly healthy and normal (psst . . . there it is again). And we also carried with us a revitalized feeling of excitement about what was happening. After getting caught up in the day-to-day details of the pregnancy, such as the decorating and whatnot, you begin to lose your focus on what is really important here. Now we knew that we had a healthy and perfect little baby boy growing inside of her. Life was good.

Julie and I each took a few copies of the ultrasound photos back to the office with us, where no one could make out the image of a baby either. "Is that the baby? That's not it, is it? I see a leg. Or is that a wing? I don't see a baby. All I see is what appears to be the Pillsbury Doughboy in a microwave."

Ahh, technology . . .

# S-E-X: A Four-Letter Word

FOR THOSE OF YOU OUT THERE waiting for me to discuss sex during pregnancy, forget it. My mother will be reading this book. And if you think I'm going to talk about my sex life in front of my mom, you're crazy. All I can say is, consult a physician. Besides, there's precious little to report. Sex gets you there, but a pregnancy takes all sport out of the bedroom. Next chapter, please . . .

# PART THREE

# Rounding Third

# Knock-Knock! Who's There?

WELL, AT THIS POINT let's assume that you've successfully survived the first two trimesters and are now comfortably ensconced in trimester number three. Well done. Your lovely bride might not be feeling quite so smug, since she's likely packed on considerable weight and she's starting to sleep less and bitch more, but those are her problems. OK, they're yours too, since you have to try to sleep next to her and you are the one most often on the listening end of her hormonal griping. Here's a doozy of a situation: Does she hold it against you yet that you can sleep soundly but she can't? Sorry, I can't help you sort that one out; there really is no way to win that particular war.

Instead, let's review what you've likely accomplished: By now you have probably decided on a name, decorated the room (though your wife will no doubt not be done with "the finishing touches" for quite some time), plotted out in your head (if not on paper) the quickest route to the hospital, bought all of those useless things that I told you not to buy in the first place, and gained sixteen pounds.

With luck, you've also now felt the baby move for the first time. This is an odd feeling at best. It's strange seeing little areas of your wife's stomach bounce up and down, and it can be a little unsettling to witness for the first time if you're not expecting it. It's a little science-fictionesque. Sometimes the baby can be moving around so furiously that it appears your wife is popping popcorn somewhere deep in her belly. Our little kicker would be most active around ten at night, when we were just settling down after a long day of working and purchasing even more useless baby-related shit that we agreed we wouldn't buy in the first place. Julie would be just ready to fall asleep when the baby's Tae Bo session would begin. One night, out of the corner of my eye I actually saw the comforter on the bed move up and down. I said, "Was that the baby?" But Julie couldn't answer. She was too busy writhing in pain and scolding our unborn son. "Quit kicking me in the ribs!" Poor kid. He hadn't even been born yet, and he was just inches away from being grounded.

I used to play a game with our little kicker. Whenever he would place his feet to a point where I could see them, I'd grab on to his foot, or at least the area of my wife's stomach that had the outline of a baby's foot. Then he'd pull his foot away and place it on another area of her stomach, and I'd grab it again. Julie would say, "Be careful! You're going to hurt him!" Hurt him? What am I, Lenny from *Of Mice and Men*? What am I going to do? Hang onto his little feet so hard that I break them? Does she really think I'm this stupid? So I kept going until either the baby tired of the game or my wife's belly was bruised and sore.

Sometimes, we would play "knock-knock" with the baby. If I hadn't seen him move around for a while, I'd lift up Julie's shirt, give her stomach a little tap and say, "Knock-knock." He'd usually answer back either with a foot to the area where I knocked or he'd give his mommy a quick punch in the ribs.

By this time in her pregnancy, your wife will undoubtedly read in a book somewhere that it is good for you to talk to your baby so they begin to become acquainted with your voice, even in the womb. The theory here is that your voice will be heard and recognized by your unborn child, then once the baby is born, they will hear a familiar voice and be comforted by this. Well that's all fine and dandy, and talking to your baby sounds like a great idea, doesn't it?

Let me tell you this. You will never in your life feel so foolish as you will when you start carrying on a conversation with your wife's midriff. "Hey there. How are you? How's my baby boy? How's my little sweetie?" You're saying all this while staring at your wife's belly button, as if your baby is going to answer back by utilizing her navel as a communications port. Well, you can be assured that this will not happen. So stop ogling her stomach waiting for an answer, and try to muster any dignity you might have left. Get off of your knees, pull your wife's blouse back down to its normal position, and resume your dinner. The waiter has the cops on the phone, and the other diners are looking at you like you have a third eye. Save the baby-daddy bonding time for when you're at home with the blinds pulled and the lights off.

From the darned books, via your wife, you'll also hear a lot of talk about playing classical music through a pair of headphones that sit directly on your wife's stomach. The music is pumped right through to your baby, who, it should be said, is probably wondering what the hell is going on. I'm not really sure what the purpose of playing this music is. Perhaps it's to get the baby prepared for listening to Muzak on the elevator at work after they bust out of the womb.

Actually, the theory is that classical music somehow magically helps children in their understanding of mathematics, an idea that I find to be a little off. I have listened to classical music ever since I was knee-high to a kitten and I can't figure 2+2 without a little help from a calculator. But maybe I was listening to the wrong composer or something. Maybe Beethoven wasn't as good at math as Mozart was, but was better at English (a subject in which I was quite advanced during my school career). But it is an extremely hysterical sight to walk into a room and witness a pair of headphones resting on your wife's belly pumping concertos or whatever program NPR happens to be running at the time directly into the womb. And you begin to feel sorry for the poor headphones, which are strained to the point where any sudden movement will send them shooting off into the atmosphere like a tightly stretched rubber band. The top of the headphones are expanded from one side of her torso clear over to the other side of Mount St. Baby. And you find this to be really funny until it dawns on you that those are *your* headphones and they are nearly stretched beyond repair! But look at it this way—if music helps the baby with his math skills, you should sacrifice your headphones so that he'll pay the bills and balance your checkbook for you.

# Back to School

AROUND THE TIME YOUR WIFE is eight months pregnant, it will be suggested to you that childbirth classes are in order. Let me rephrase that: You will be *told* to get in the car with your wife and get to childbirth class. My advice to you: Don't fight it. Most men I know groan at the idea of going to these things, and I did too. But veteran that I am, I'm pleased to report that these classes are actually quite helpful. For first-time parents, childbirth is an ambiguous mystery that is frightening and confusing, wouldn't you agree? I mean, you can read about it, watch videos on the subject, visualize what your experience might be like (which you're always wrong about, by the way), and hear all your friends' horror stories. But until you actually experience childbirth, you cannot fathom what it is really like.

Truth be told, childbirth classes are invaluable. Seriously. They give you the opportunity to focus on the impending experience, trade pregnancy stories, piss and moan with other parents-to-be, and learn a handy little breathing method called Lamaze, which emphasizes pain management through relaxation and breathing exercises (big points for you if you know this definition before the class, so pay attention here, boys). The instructors will show you how, by simply breathing and keeping oxygen moving to the brain, you can diminish the amount of pain experienced during labor, thereby eliminating the need for pain medication. Of course, this is utter nonsense. During labor, if you try telling your wife in midcontraction, "Just breathe, honey. You don't need the epidural. Just breathe. There. You feel better now, don't you?" you will limp for quite a long time. So don't buy into the whole "breathing will make it all better" bullshit. Just do what you've done for the last thirty-odd weeks: nod, smile, and say, "OK." Just pretend to go along with it. You paid for the class already, and there was nothing good on TV tonight anyway.

Aside from the breathing nonsense, you'll also get to watch videos of an actual childbirth at childbirth class. Good times, right? No doubt you've seen a few Hollywood movies where an actress like Jennifer Aniston is covered in fake sweat but her lipstick remains perfectly intact, she starts screaming like the baby is eating her from the inside, and within five minutes a baby pops out covered in grape jelly, looking like a flawlessly formed and healthy six-month-old. The head is perfectly round, the mouth is covered in formula, and its size three diaper needs to be changed. It's ridiculous, but you believed it because you've never been involved in an actual childbirth. So you're thinking, "OK, I can handle that." Well, that is nothing like what you'll witness on this particular video.

First of all, the childbirth class childbirth video quality is second only to a Russ Meyer film taped in his garage. The lighting is bad, the camera jumps around, and there isn't a Jennifer Aniston in sight. Hell, there isn't even a John Aniston in sight. But to be fair, this *is* an amateur video made for educational purposes, and not for Hollywood. It's just not what you're accustomed to. Brace yourself.

But the worst part is the camera angle. The videographer has the lens of the camera pointed directly into the woman's birth canal! You are nose-to-nose (so to speak) with this stranger's gaping vagina. Now at this point, you might want to take notice of something: Your wife's face. She finds this to be a beautiful thing. Any other time, if you told your wife that you paid money to watch a video starring some

strange woman's vagina, she'd be furious and you'd get to re-
visit the "Hotel Couch" for a night or two. But suddenly, it's
beautiful because it's childbirth.

(Just a side note here. . . . Can you imagine walking
down the street and running into this woman from the
video? What's the protocol here? Do you stop her and tell her
that you've seen her crotch on a video screen? Do you compliment her on a job well done, and perhaps suggest a bush
trimming? Personally, I think I'd just keep walking. . . . )

Your wife's opinion as to how beautiful an experience
this is quickly changes once she sees the amount of pain
our new friend on the video is in. The video shows the
doctor stretching the woman in order to make room for
the baby to come out, and you can hear every woman in
the room react to this. Some of them cry. Some grab themselves in a protective manner. Some of them call their
lawyers on their cell phones to see if they can get out of
this whole childbirth process. Pain is a motivator. That is,
it motivates you to change your stance by becoming pro-
drugs and anti-Lamaze. My wife asked if she could have a
shunt installed *now*, so the epidural could be dumped in at
a moment's notice.

The other interesting and helpful things you might
learn (I say "might" because there's no guarantee that you'll
retain all this info) include how to diaper your newborn,

how to feed him, burp him, and bathe him. While these sound like extremely elementary tasks, you have to keep in mind that people in these classrooms (such as myself) have never changed a diaper in their lives.

Overall, I'd say that I found the course to be well worth the money. It helped prepare us for parenthood, if only a little bit. And since we scheduled our classes at a time that was right after work, it kept us out of rush hour traffic. Bonus!

# Co-ed Showers:
# Not What You're Thinking

THERE ARE A FEW THINGS IN LIFE that clearly do not work well together. These things should be kept separated, just as the good Lord intended them to be. Things such as: church and state, beer and chocolate (regardless of what my wife says), peanut butter and mayonnaise, and most important, *men and baby showers*.

I'm sorry, but certain gatherings should involve solely men *or* women, but not both. Bachelor parties: men. Bachelorette parties: women. Poker night: guys. Lingerie party: gals. See how it works? One final comparison and then we'll move on. Getting together for wings and football at Hooters: men. Baby showers: women.

Men's attendance at baby showers is a phenomenon that probably began sometime during the Clinton administration, known as the "Pussification Period" in America. Men were taught to get in touch with their feminine side and embrace the diversities of men and women. This apparently included having to go to baby showers.

I hated going to these baby showers, as would any red-blooded heterosexual man. Call me a sexist pig. Send me to Hell. Whatever. As long as I never have to attend one of these damn things again, I'll be content to spend all eternity with my chestnuts roasting on an open fire.

Now the co-ed baby shower, in theory, seems to be a good idea. I mean, you go register at a store for all kinds of baby-related items (bottles, clothes, diapers, shampoos, etc.). And people are supposed to go buy these items *for you*, and you get to eat snack foods and watch the goodies roll in. So it seems like a good idea . . . in theory. Then again, communism is a good idea "in theory." I think we all know how well *that* works.

So am I comparing a baby shower to communism? Well . . . no. Not really. I couldn't back that one up if I had to. But the fact remains that these parties are boring. They feature a lot of giggling women eating dainty little snacks. And all the while they're "Ooing" and "Aahing" at tiny little clothes that have pictures of puppies and *Sesame Street* characters on them.

Despite my warnings, it's inevitable that you'll be duped into attending a couple of these events, so it's important that you understand what you're in for (see if this just doesn't sound like a thrill a minute):

1. You'll have to sit in the center of the room next to your wife, even though you'll try to sit in the corner, away from everyone else, and eat three times your body weight in sausage balls.

2. You'll remain sitting completely still with your hands folded as your wife opens up the gifts, straining to smile as if you're actually enjoying this.

3. You'll say things like, "Well look at that. Isn't that cute? Thank you so much. This will help out a great deal"—even though you won't have a clue what some of these items are.

4. You'll hold up each unwrapped gift between you and your wife so that twenty women can take pictures of you looking like an idiot, proudly displaying a gift that you're probably holding upside down since you still don't know what the hell it is.

5. You'll do one of those closed-mouth yawns that isn't fooling anybody.

6. You'll load up your car with ten tons of crap that you didn't ask for in the first place and three items that you actually registered for. (No one ever checks your registry, by the way. So why even fill one out? People simply buy you what they think you should have. Therefore you receive thirty-six bottles of baby shampoo, five copies of the same Elmo video, three bouncy seats, and *zero* diapers, the one item you will truly need every day for the next two years or so, which is why you listed them on your registry.)

7. You'll go home and drink a beer right in front of your wife and won't feel guilty about it in the least. By God, she owes you at least that much. . . .

Yes, it's true. You will be forced into going to these stupid girly events. I'm sorry. There's just no way out of it. I tried everything short of faking a seizure, but I still had to go. So if by some miracle you find a loophole and are able to get out of attending a baby shower, may I suggest writing a book on the topic? A book on weaseling out of baby showers would sell like hotcakes. And men all over the world will probably register for it when they're preparing for their own pussification party (a.k.a. co-ed baby shower).

# Ready? Set? Wait!

ASSUMING YOUR WIFE doesn't go into early labor, the day will finally come when she reaches the forty-week point in her pregnancy. And as we discussed earlier, this is when the baby is supposed to make its appearance. This is the stage when every time your wife so much as clears her throat, you'll jump up to go start the car and head to the nearest hospital. But nothing happens, and you wait. And you'll continue to wait. And while you're waiting, you'll wonder, "Isn't this supposed to be over by now? We've been waiting for forty weeks and we still don't have anything to fill these tiny little outfits with." Too bad childbirth isn't like Domino's Pizza. Wouldn't it be great to have a guarantee like, "We deliver in forty weeks or your hospital bill is on us!" Well, you could try asking someone in the billing office at the hospital if they'd consider this deal. But you'll more than likely have your knuckles crushed with an adding machine.

So if it's been forty weeks like we read about in all those books, where the hell is the baby? Well, apparently the kid doesn't have a calendar pinned up inside the womb. Because in most cases, first-time mothers will go beyond their due date without going into labor. This is what happened in our case. And chances are you'll be playing "The Waiting Game" as well, which is kind of like "The Crying Game," but without the cross-dressing.

Anxiety and impatience aside, it's not as though this is a boring period. A few odd things start to show up around forty weeks. Indeed, an interesting phenomenon that occurs during this time is known as "swelling." At first, this swelling can cause great concern to you and especially to your wife, who is the one experiencing it and the one who has seemingly and suddenly blown up to several times her already bloated pregnancy size. But don't worry, this is perfectly natural. As I understand it, the swelling (or edema) results from the extra blood that she acquired during her pregnancy. During your wife's pregnancy, she develops growing pressure on her pelvic veins and vena cava (a large vein deep in the body that receives blood from the lower limbs). This causes her circulation to slow down, so her blood pools, and there you have the swelling. Pressure from the pooled blood forces water to go down into the tissues of her feet and ankles. That water is fluid that would normally be *in* her body and now is simply displaced. But sometimes pregnant women also retain excess water, which adds to the swelling. So it is perfectly normal and really nothing to worry about.

Easy for the doctors to say! This part of "nothing to worry" about is creepy because swelling and bloating doesn't happen only in the ankles and fingers. Perhaps your wife's swelling will manifest itself in her face. Yes, her face might show signs of swelling in places that you probably didn't even know were capable of bloating, such as the nose. Whose nose swells up for no good reason? One second my wife's nose was as cute and petite as it always had been, and the next thing I knew, she turned around and it looked like she had been involved in a bare-fisted prize fight with Philo Beddoe in *Every Which Way But Loose*.

Or maybe her ankles will swell to the point where she can no longer wear her own shoes. This is why you see a lot of pregnant women walking around barefoot. If they attempt to squeeze into their shoes, their ankles start spilling over the sides, giving the appearance of baking bread in their boots.

So you immediately reach for one of those books like *What to Expect When You're Exploding* or whatever, to see what you can do to cure or at least minimize the swelling, and what does it tell you? "Drink plenty of water." Would someone please tell me how the hell drinking six to eight glasses of water actually *reduces* the amount of water your body retains? That's like telling someone to fill their tires with air to reduce the amount of air in the tires. This makes no sense to me at all, and frankly, we didn't find that it helped that much. The one thing that helped in my wife's situation (and will perhaps help your bloated lover) is relaxing. If she puts her feet up, that will help out quite a bit. Another good way to help her is to lay the swollen princess on her left side. This seems to help a great deal if you couple it with cutting down on salty foods.

And if the waiting and swelling aren't enough fun for you, there is also the fact that your very grumpy bride will no longer be able to sleep, as the baby has grown so big that it is nearly impossible for her to get any rest at all. So she's swollen, tired, gassy, in constant back pain, cranky, bruised on the inside from the baby making her into a human punching bag, constipated, suffering from hemorrhoids, still gassy, getting false contractions, frightened about the impending labor pains, frantically packing and unpacking her hospital suitcase because she keeps forgetting to put shit in there, still freakin' gassy, and just a joy to be around in general. So whatever you do, stay out of the way. Do absolutely nothing to piss this woman off. Would you poke a growling lion with a stick? Of course not. Just do what you've been doing all along. Smile, nod, and say "OK" to whatever she says. Trust me. You'll thank me later.

# PART FOUR

# . . . And Baby Makes Three

# Daydream Believer

THERE ARE TWO SCENARIOS that I'm sure have run through your head the entire duration of this pregnancy ordeal. At least there were for me, and some daddy friends of mine told me that they had similar thoughts, especially toward the end of the pregnancy. These thoughts will haunt you right up until the time when the baby is a week old and you realize that neither of these things happened. The first fantasy/nightmare probably involves something along these lines:

Your wife calls you at work from across town and says, "My water broke! The baby's head is coming out, and I can't control the urge to push! There's no answer at 9-1-1, and you're the only person who can right this situation!" So you jump into your car, drive down the highway in the breakdown lane with your hazard lights on, doing somewhere around 176 mph. A cop pulls you over (damn those pesky cops), you explain the situation to him, and the *now* very nice officer gives you an escort all the way home. (Maybe this year you *will* contribute to the Policemen Charity Ball.) So you get home, rush into the house, boil some water, roll up your sleeves, and catch the baby as it flies out of your wife's crotch. You're a hero. You're offered the key to your city but must decline the Nobel Prize because of a previous engagement. (Alternate ending to this scenario: You don't make it home in time and your baby is born right there on your living room floor, making a mess of the carpeting. Still, you're a hero because the baby is healthy and you managed to steam clean the carpeting. A national morning show anchorwoman wants to interview you the next day about the amazing cleaning product you used.) End of fantasy.

The next daydream is more like a nightmare. It places you in bed, sometime around four in the morning. You're deep in Slumberland, sleeping more soundly than you ever have in your life. Your wife's water breaks, and she starts feeling intense labor pains. She's doing her breathing exercises, which surprisingly aren't doing a damn thing for her.

She reaches over to shake you, but you won't wake up. She starts screaming your name, begging you to wake up and help her. But you continue to snore, so she is forced to go through this ordeal all by herself. Three hours later, you awaken to find stained sheets and your newborn lying next to your wife, who has passed out from the pain. (*This* particular nightmare kept me from sleeping a wink for the last couple of weeks of Julie's pregnancy.)

Well, never fear. Neither of these scenes remotely resembles what will actually happen. But try not to sleep from now until the baby is born, just to be on the safe side. . . .

# The Arrival

I DIDN'T EXPERIENCE one of those moments where my wife looks at me and says, "It's time." She never showed any of the traditional signs of labor. Her water never broke on its own. She didn't dilate to more than one centimeter. She experienced mild false labor pains (called "practice contractions," helpful as a concept only if you know they aren't the real thing), but it was never anything so alarming that it made us hop into the car and get rolling to the nearest maternity ward. Our little guy was in no rush to be born. He was content just being in his mother's womb, and I can't really say that I blame him. This was the beginning of January, it was colder than a witch's tit in a brass bra, and he was floating around in a 98 degree hot tub. He was getting all the nutrition he needed through the umbilical cord, and it was nice and dark in there in case he wanted to catch a quick nap. Plus, he was getting a free ride wherever he went. Why would he want to come out? I know I'd have been hanging out there beside him if only he wouldn't have hogged the umbilical cord. So once it was determined that Julie was far enough overdue (if she'd been in charge, this determination would have come months earlier), the doctor decided to pursue the alternate course and induce labor.

Inducing labor isn't all that bad, especially for us guys, since we're not the ones dealing with all the pain. It's really the ideal situation. An induced labor is planned out a couple of days in advance, so you know exactly when you need to be at the hospital. Bonus #1: This eliminates the need to race across town, flying through school zones, cutting through parking lots, and sideswiping a nun or something. You can just take your time getting there. But I gotta tell you, this is one long car ride. Sure, there's no screaming in pain or breaking water. But it's a long, long ride. Julie and I sat in total and complete silence for the better part of the 25 minute car trip. We just held hands and each prayed in silence. I mean, this was *it*. This was the big moment that we'd been awaiting for the last 287 days. (Yes, I counted. And frankly, it seemed like longer.) We were going to be

parents in just a matter of hours. And I think we both realized at the same time that *we were not even remotely ready
for this*. No matter how much planning, decorating, and
reading we had done (and God knows we did plenty of all
these things), we were now trying to figure out how to just
call time-out. "Hi, Doc. Yeah, it's Julie Crider. Listen, we've
been thinking, and we've decided to just forget this whole
thing. OK? No? Oh, I see. Not possible, huh? All right
then. Great. See you shortly."

Bonus #2: When you walk into the hospital to have
labor induced, the doctor has already scheduled for your
pregnant beauty to come in. This means that she doesn't
have to go through a lengthy check-in process. You just
walk in, tell them you're here, and they give your wife a
room. It's kind of like she is staying at the Hilton (if the
staff at the Hilton walked in and took a look at her vagina
every hour or so, that is). This is really, in my opinion, a
much easier and civilized way of dealing with the first part
of the birthing process. Not that this is a completely worry
free situation. Trust me, there are no more bonuses, and
you will have plenty of nerve-wracking moments in the
not-so-distant future.

It all goes something like this . . .

As you enter the room, you will begin to notice your
surroundings. You see a nice big hospital bed, one of those

bright surgical lights resting right above the bed, a nice little end table with a lamp and a phone right next to the bed,
a TV with a VCR (and in some cases a CD or DVD player
is available), and a private bathroom with a bathtub/shower
combo. And you're thinking, *Dude, this really is starting to
look like the Hilton. Sweet!* Then you start to notice some of
the subtle differences between a five-star hotel suite and
this hospital room. For instance, most fancy hotels do not
offer machines that monitor the mother and the baby's
heart rate, an IV stand directly behind the bed, and a table
with various medically related tools. And even the seediest
of hotels will generally have something comfortable to sleep
on for more than one person. That's when you begin to ask,
"Um . . . where will I be sleeping?"

At this point, the nurse directs you to what appears to
be the refrigerator from your college dorm room. It's a little brown box that you probably thought was either a
minifridge for an honor bar or a dishwasher. Instead, you
find that it stores a tiny cot complete with worn-out, rusted
springs, a lumpy mattress, and the musty smell of the last
guy who rested his head on this bacteria trap that is dou-
bling as a bed. And you're thinking to yourself, *This can't be
where I'm sleeping. Can it?*

Good news: The universally nasty cot is not where
you'll be sleeping. Because, you see, you won't be sleeping at

all. I mean, you will be lying down on this God-forsaken contraption. But you won't be sleeping. Between your nerves about the impending birth, the hospital staff that comes and goes twelve times a night to check your wife's vitals (more on this later), and trying to figure out what exactly is poking you in the back through this mattress, you won't get any sleep at all. However, you should be used to this feeling by now, since you stopped sleeping a week ago because you were afraid your wife would plop out this kid and not be able to awaken you for help. But never fear. You'll get plenty of sleep after the baby is born. Ha ha ha ha ha ha ha ha ha ha. Oh . . . That was a good one. You may not get that joke yet, but just wait. You'll get it soon enough.

Moving right along. It's at about this time that you can expect the nurse to hand your wife one of those oh-so-fashionable hospital gowns. You know the one I'm talking about: it covers the entire front of your wife's body from her shoulders down to about midshin but leaves her back and entire ass out for all the world to see. With all of the medical advances we have in this day and age, can't we do something about this? Perhaps make a full-length gown that covers the entire body but has a zipper? Or better yet, how about a one-piece set of footed pajamas with a tear-away crotch so we can still get the baby out, yet somehow allow the mother to retain a certain amount of dignity?

But I digress. Once she has donned this gown and now looks sufficiently like something out of one of Mr. Blackwell's nightmares, the soon-to-be mother hops into the hospital bed, has a lubricant applied to her stomach and then an external fetal monitor attached atop the lubricated area. This monitor will send signals of the baby's pulse and other vital information to the aforementioned monitoring machines behind the bed. Then an IV is inserted into your wife's forearm or hand, supplying her with all the vodka she will need to get through this procedure. (Just kidding. Thought I'd see if you were paying attention.) Actually, the IV delivers Pitocin or a similar synthetic form of the hormone oxytocin. This drug is used as a means of speeding up the labor, causing your wife to contract more. These contractions will help dilate her cervix to ten centimeters, making it possible to push the baby's head out. But it doesn't happen immediately, and the amount of time it takes to fully dilate is completely dependent on the individual situation. For Julie, it took about seven hours to go from one centimeter to ten centimeters. It takes some women longer, and some women squirt out their kid in as little as two hours.

Here's the routine for those of you checking in with an already laboring wife: She won't be hopping onto any bed, she'll throw herself onto it. She won't need Pitocin, because Mother Nature will take care of increasing contractions and stretching the ol' cervix without the vodka, er, Pitocin. All the rest: the same. So it's now just a matter of time. During the interval between the moment when the Pitocin is introduced into her body and when it takes effect, you do what you've been doing for a few weeks now. You play the waiting game again, which you are more than a little accustomed to and are completely sick of by now. So to pass the time, you'll watch some TV, make a few phone calls, maybe talk to your spouse (though chances are you're both trying hard not to focus on what's about to happen). Perhaps you'll even try to get some sleep on the evil cot from Hell.

But even if this cot were comfortable, you wouldn't be able to rest. Hospitals are lousy places to catch up on your sleep. The room isn't dark enough, you can hear people walking up and down the hall outside your door, you hear what sounds like professional movers running couches from one side of the hospital to the other over and over again, and you hear announcements over the PA system outside saying things like, "All personnel . . . Code Blue, Room 203. Code Blue." And your first thought is, "What's our room number again? 2 . . . 0 . . . 6! Whew. Thank God."

And then, as I alluded to before, there's the issue of nurses walking in at all times of the day and night to check your wife's vitals. They check to see if she has dilated at all, they check her temperature and the baby's heart rate, and they refill her IV bags if needed. In some cases, they even wake up a patient in order to give them a sleeping pill! What the hell?

One last indignity before the nurse leaves: She'll strap a mechanical blood pressure cuff to your wife's arm. This contraption will give blood pressure readings every few minutes. This damn thing is about as whisper quiet as a dump truck in dire need of a tune-up. So even if you do start to doze off after the nurse leaves the room, this machine will perk you right back up into your state of misery.

At this juncture, I know what you're thinking: How are you supposed to be at your supportive best if the hospital staff won't give you a moment's peace and quiet? How can you be expected to "be there" and be your wife's "advocate" if you've had less sleep than you did the night of your bachelor party? Unfortunately, I'm here to tell you that there's no use fighting it, man. These things have been going on since before you and I were born and the procedures aren't likely to change in this lifetime. I found that the only way to stop myself from screaming for some peace and quiet or throttling the nurse was to remind myself that Julie had it worse . . . she was about to push a human being out of her vagina, the equivalent—she was fond of pointing out—of pushing a bowling ball out of my urethra.

# Let's Get Ready to Rumble!

AT THIS POINT YOU MAY BE ASKING how you might be able to tell exactly when the Pitocin has kicked in. Well, there are several ever-so-subtle telltale signs that your bride is indeed in labor. You may notice even the slightest changes in her behavior, such as:

1. Uncontrollable screaming
2. Crying
3. Cursing that would make a sailor blush
4. The bending of the metal bed frame with her bare hands

5. The fact that she has pulled all the sheets off the bed using only her butt cheeks, where the sheets are currently lodged

So this, coupled with the fact that she is saying over and over, "I'm having a contraction! I'm having a contraction!" might give you a clue that nature has begun to take its course. Another salient characteristic of this stage of labor is your wife telling you that nothing you're doing is right. Some women scream things like, "I hate you! You did this to me!" Or they try to physically hurt the father, just so he'll be suffering as much as they are. In my case, my wife just nit-picked about little things. She wasn't allowed to eat or drink anything at this point. She could only suck on ice chips. So being the supportive husband that I am, I hand-fed her the ice chips. She told me that the way I was giving her the ice was driving her crazy. I'm still not sure what this meant, but I was offended. Here I was trying to help her out by keeping her hydrated, and I was catching hell for it. In retrospect, I guess I got off light. At least she didn't grab me by the gonads and scream obscenities at me. But I was prepared. I had brought earplugs and an athletic cup and you'd be well advised to do the same.

Now if your wife's water has not yet broken when labor gets under way, the doctor will come in and break it for her, as if she isn't uncomfortable enough in her current situation. To do this, the doctor takes what appears to be a hooked crochet needle and jams it up into your wife. I know that might not sound tactful, but there is just no delicate way to put it to make you feel any better. I'm not going to try to hide the truth from you. I haven't up to this point, and by God I'm not about to start now. The doctor jams that damn thing up there and breaks the water. When Julie's doctor did this, she told Julie that she might notice a slight trickling stream of water coming out, and I couldn't help but think one of those tabletop water fountains. You know the ones I mean. They come complete with little polished rocks, and they create soothing sounds of trickling water. How I will ever picture one of those things quite the same again, I don't know.

In case you're wondering, breaking the water is helpful and sometimes necessary because doing so helps allow the woman's body to dilate faster. And this is a good thing. The faster she starts dilating, the faster we can get this crazy lady some good old-fashioned drugs!

If your wife learned anything in those childbirth classes, it was probably that she wanted to have the epidural. As she contracts and continues to dilate, the window for drugs will open up. Most doctors recommend not getting the epidural until the screaming lady on the bed has dilated to at least three centimeters. After that point, how-ever (and perhaps well before), there's probably no stopping your old lady from insisting on having the epidural admin-istered stat. You see (and in the event that you didn't glean this at childbirth classes), an epidural decreases the sensa-tion in the lower areas of your wife's body while allowing her to remain awake. Medication is delivered through a catheter inserted into the membrane that surrounds the spinal cord. In order for the anesthesiologist to perform the epidural, your miserable and groaning wife must lie curled in the fetal position (no pun intended) on her side while he injects a needle into her lower back, passes the catheter through it, then pulls out the needle. The doc then places some tape on and around the catheter to hold it in place. This allows for the medication to flow from an IV bag to the bloodstream as needed. All of this sounds incredibly painful, but in our case, my wife said that she never even felt the needle going in. She was too concerned about hav-ing to be curled up in a ball while going through a con-traction. She said that was the worst part of the epidural experience by far.

After the epidural kicks in, things start to relax a bit. My wife was in absolutely no pain at all after the drugs began working. I believe you could have chopped off her feet with a butter knife and she wouldn't have flinched.

Whoever invented the epidural should receive some kind of award. Julie even took a nap after the pain subsided! Of course, I did not nap—that cot made doing so simply impossible.

Once Julie was no longer hurting, her body relaxed, and she was able to make it to the full ten centimeters that would be needed to get our kid out. When the nurse last checked her, she was completely dilated, ready to start pushing, and the doctor was called in. It was "showtime." I was about to officially become a daddy. And I couldn't have been more terrified. . . .

# Make Like a Baby and "Head Out"

ONCE THE ACTUAL PUSHING PROCESS BEGAN, I started to take my designated role of Coach pretty seriously. I was giving Julie words of encouragement and handing out helpful advice, such as "Push!" I was also counting to ten a lot. That's how many seconds they ask the mothers to push, so I was acting as a human clock. This was about as useful as I had ever felt during the entire pregnancy. At last I was getting to do something, even if it was just counting out loud. I had said the numbers 1 through 10 so many times I was beginning to sound like an episode of *Sesame Street*.

After forty-five minutes or so of pushing (Julie) and counting (me), Ryan's head made its debut. This, I understood from some of the reading I actually did bother to do, was called "crowning." Then the doctor said to me, "Look at his hair. I think he has reddish hair," and she began touching the baby's head and sort of petting it. Now I'm wondering what the baby was thinking at this moment. I mean, his entire body was being squeezed out of an opening only slightly larger than the average garden hose, the top of his head was feeling the cold outside air for the very first time, and some stranger who he couldn't see was petting his scalp. This has to be an odd sensation. All the while, he kept hearing some moron counting to ten every thirty seconds or so. This poor kid had a rough day already, and he wasn't even born yet!

As more and more of my son entered my realm of vision, Julie continued to push and I kept counting. But I found that as his head popped out and his face became discernible, I started counting faster. My adrenaline was pumping, my eyes were wide open and flooded with tears. I was excited. So I went from counting in even, ten second intervals to sounding like a first-time auctioneer selling off some swampland in Florida. I was stuttering, stumbling over words, and forgetting what number comes after five. Eventually, the doctor had to slow me down, and she even started doing the counting herself. So I just held Julie's hand and watched as my son, my baby boy, my new reason for being, began to appear right before my now-very-weepy eyes.

The doctor said to Julie, "OK, I'm going to need you to stop pushing, because the baby is starting to come out really fast now." But it was too late at that point. Julie, who was still completely numb from the epidural, had no idea how hard she was pushing or even if she was pushing at all. So even as the doctor was requesting that she no longer push, the baby came shooting out. The doctor did kind of a one-arm catch, and that was the end of it. Our son was born.

Ryan Michael Crider was born at 1:57 p.m. on January 6, 2000. He weighed six pounds, eleven ounces. He came out kicking and crying, and the very first thing he ever did in this world was pee all over the doctor. That's my boy. Defying authority already.

# The Angry Raisin

**AS SOON AS RYAN** had officially arrived, the doctor held him up and said to me, "All right, Dad. You're on! Cut the cord!" Now, we had discussed this months earlier. The doctor and Julie had both asked me whether or not I was going to cut the umbilical cord, to which I responded, "Hell no." I mean, isn't there someone who works in the hospital who is more qualified to do this? What am I paying the doctor for? Do you want me to perform a quick heart operation while I'm here? This whole cord-cutting thing seemed like a serious medical procedure, and I just didn't think I'd be the man for the job. I'm a bit of a klutz. The last thing I felt that I needed to be doing was handling sharp objects near this newborn. But since the doctor had now cornered me and kind of put me on the spot, I finally agreed. I mean, I didn't want my son to think his dad was a wuss. So I grabbed the scalpel in my shaking, sweating hands and cut the cord. In case you're wondering, it felt very tough. The texture was similar to that of a wet rubber hose. And it tasted like chicken.

In case you're considering your own ability or desire to cut your child's cord, it might help you to know that I'm glad that the doctor talked me into doing this. It wasn't nearly as bad as I thought it was going to be. And sure, it's a symbolic gesture that separates the child from the mother, making him into an individual. But it is also the first time that I bonded with my son. In a way, I was sort of freeing him and readying him for the world. (You're still weirded out by that "tasted like chicken" comment, aren't you? It was just a joke. Gee whiz, lighten up. . . . )

After the cord-cutting incident, one of the nurses cleaned Ryan up a little bit and placed him on his mother's chest. This was a rather amazing moment, because as they laid him down he was crying and screaming, and I can't say as I blame him. He was probably cold, it was too bright in the room, the nurse who toweled him off also stuck a bulb aspirator in his nose and mouth to clear them out, and he had just humiliated himself by peeing on a perfect stranger.

But as soon as he heard his mommy's voice, he seemed to settle down. He seemed to be comforted by a familiar voice, and he was starting to put two and two together. It was as if he was thinking, "Oh, OK. I recognize that voice. You're that Mommy person I've been listening to all this time. Wow, that's weird. I had pictured you to be taller." Julie covered his little face so that the light wouldn't be so bright, and just talked to him in a soothing soft voice until she had calmed him down in the way that only a mother could. It was like she had been doing this for years. I was awestruck. Then Julie, with a statement so perfect it was as if it were scripted, looked at her newborn and said, "Welcome to the world." Then she kissed Ryan for the very first time.

My memory of the next period is a little blurry (remember, I'd had very little sleep and emotions were running high). I know that Julie and I studied the little creature that had been plopped down on her chest for about twenty minutes. We counted his fingers and toes, looked at his perfectly sculpted little fingernails, ran our fingers through the little hair that he had, and just tried to absorb him. After getting over the "oh shit" moment months before, both Julie and I had of course dreamed of this day and attempted to picture what Ryan would look like when he first came out. I've got to tell you that this kid looked nothing like I thought he would. I'm not even really sure what I thought he'd look like, but it wasn't anything like this. He had the whole alien-shaped head that most newborns have, and the area from his eyebrows to his chin was only about two inches long! He was just a tiny, scrunched-up looking person. He looked like an angry raisin. It's not that I thought he was ugly, by any means. He was absolutely adorable. The entire situation was just surreal. I defy you to describe it otherwise when your turn comes.

After we had looked over every inch of this poor boy's body, the nurses whisked him over to another area of the room to perform the "Apgar test." The Apgar test is a way of measuring a newborn's initial condition and response to any resuscitative efforts. As the nurse looks over the baby, she can usually tell what's going on just by how the baby is responding. But to make it official, they run through the test and give the baby a score. (Oh, God. His first test. I hope he studied while he was in there or he's grounded. . . . ) The nurse assigns each category a score between 0 and 2. Afterward, the scores are totaled. The closer to 10 you get, the better off the baby is. Incidentally, Ryan got a 9. I guess he didn't stick the landing or something.

Shortly after our initial bonding period and Ryan's first pop quiz of sorts, he was taken away to the nursery. At this time they tied off his umbilical cord stump and gave him his first little bath, and he was clad in his very first diaper. While he was away, Julie was moved to a recovery room, where she received her first meal in over 24 hours and got some much-needed rest. This freed me up to make all the phone calls I needed to make to friends and family, filling everyone in on all the pertinent details of the birth. Ryan's weight, length, and time of birth, the duration of the actual "active labor," the status of his health and his mother's, and various other fine points of the day. Still no sleep for me.

Then of course I had to field the question, "Who does he look like?" Well, I didn't know quite how to answer this. I mean, from the very moment you lay eyes on your child, you kind of start looking at every part of their body to see whom he resembles. He had my chin, but Julie's cheeks. He had wide hands like me, with Julie's long and slender fingers. He had reddish hair that would have come from Julie's side of the family. His feet resembled my grandfather's, and his penis looked just like Julie's (just another attention check there). So instead of going into all that over the phone, I just said something like, "He looks like the both of us." This seemed to satisfy the other person on the phone, and I was then able to move on to re-answer the same obligatory questions from the next person I called.

Just as we were catching our breath and getting caught up on our rest, the visitors started flowing in. This was my cue to become public relations director and, incidentally, to steer visitors away from my exhausted, slightly disoriented wife. (Take my advice and try to do the same. You and she don't know this yet, but these few days in the hospital are very likely the last few sane days you'll have for quite some time.) I'd take well-wishers by the room where the action happened just a few short hours earlier. Then I'd walk them over to the nursery, where we could look at my son through the glass. I've always found this viewing room system to be a little weird. I mean, it's as if we're walking through a zoo and we enter the Homo sapiens exhibit. I about half expected to encounter a tour guide. ". . . And if you look over to your right, you should observe that we have four brand new baby humans that have just arrived here at the zoo. Now as we pass by, be sure to notice their alien-shaped heads. And just so you will have something to look forward to, these children will be the next batch of people who will one day cut you off in traffic, get your order wrong at the drive-thru, marry your daughters without your consent, and place you in an old folks' home. Very well then. Let's head to the aquarium."

# Tarred and Weathered

I HAD NEVER IN ALL OF MY YEARS changed a diaper until the day after my son was born. I was an only child, so I never had any younger siblings to look after. I never had a baby-sitting job growing up, either. So the closest I ever came to changing a baby is when I strapped a diaper on a teddy bear I had gotten Ryan before he was born, just to see if I could do it. The diaper fell off the teddy bear after about three seconds, and then it inexplicably caught fire. So I was a little apprehensive about when I would change a real diaper for the first time. I mean, if I couldn't keep a diaper on a stuffed animal that generally doesn't fidget around much, how would I be able to accomplish the task on a squirming infant?

When the golden moment finally arrived, Julie was lying down in her hospital bed, holding Ryan. She looked over at me and said, "I think somebody poo-pooed." After a quick self-check, I realized she wasn't talking about me. So I volunteered to be the one to change what was not only my first diaper but also my son's very first poopy diaper. At the time, we had a few people in the room with us, and I asked them all to leave. You'll understand this when your time comes, believe me. I was nervous enough; I didn't need an audience at this very moment to intimidate me further.

The room cleared of potential backseat drivers, I grabbed a fresh diaper and some cotton balls (you shouldn't use diaper wipes for the first couple of weeks—did you know that? Take note!). As I opened up the baby's diaper, I had my first encounter with a little substance called meconium.

Until becoming a father, I always believed that Meconium was the name of the guy who invented the radio. But as it turns out, meconium is a thick, sticky, tar-looking stool that the baby passes the first few days after birth, and Guglielmo Marconi was a short Italian inventor with a lot of time on his hands.

Meconium is digested residue of swallowed amniotic fluid, and it is incredibly gross. It looked like black tar shooting out of my newborn's ass. I said, "Julie, at any time during your pregnancy did you drink melted tires?" So I held up his little legs and wiped him using ten times his body weight in cotton balls. When I was finished cleaning him up, I was pretty darn proud of myself. Seeing as how I'd never done anything like that before, I did a good job. I mean, you could've eaten off this kid's butt. It was just that clean.

I opened up the new diaper, placed it under his little bottom, and immediately more meconium came flying out of the child. It startled me so badly that I jumped back about three feet. Then I took a deep breath, grabbed a new diaper and more freakin' cotton balls, and started the whole process all over again.

# PART FIVE

# Welcome Home

# Speed Demon

NORMALLY, I SIMPLY cannot be bothered to adhere to speed limits. I just can't seem to do it. I've tried, I really have. But the whole concept of speed limits just seems unconstitutional somehow. Would the founding fathers of this great land be happy that our government was placing these restrictions on us? I'd say not. Generally speaking, I will average five to seven miles per hour over the limit.

While driving the car home from the hospital with my newborn son, however, things had changed. On this particular trip, I handled the vehicle more slowly than an octogenarian who had died behind the wheel six miles back. Amish people were passing me and giving me the finger.

But speeders be damned; I was taking no chances with my new family. So even though it would take us an hour and a half to drive 25 miles, we would all get home in one piece.

When we finally arrived at the house, I walked around to the passenger side so I could take my son out of his car seat. Not so I could open the door gallantly for my bride. Hey, priorities had changed.

The image of Ryan strapped into this contraption is one that I will not soon forget. With the five-point safety harness in place, Ryan looked like a miniature fighter pilot. He resembled Snoopy when he was pretending to be the World War One Flying Ace. All he needed was the helmet, goggles, and scarf. And a machine gun. And a plane. OK, so maybe he didn't look so much like a fighter pilot as he did a very small boy in a car seat.

Bringing a baby into a house for the first time is a long and arduous process. At least that's how it was for us. We had to be sure that Ryan was secure enough in his car seat so that when we detached the seat from its base he didn't come flying out of the seat and plop down in the yard like a bag of pudding. So even though we had checked to ensure that his harness was properly attached at least four times before we left the hospital, we double-checked before getting him out of the car. Then, since he was sleeping (kids like cars, take note), I felt that we had to go creeping and tip-toeing into the house so as not to wake him. In my extremely short tenure as a father, I had already learned that a sleeping baby is a good baby, so I was taking every precaution to keep him in this state of unconsciousness. I looked like a rookie in the bomb squad carrying my first suspicious package out of the post office or something, moving at a snail's pace with a terrified look on my face and beads of sweat rolling down my cheek. And I know I looked this way, because as if this process wasn't taking long enough, I had to pause briefly outside the house to pose for the picture that my proud father-in-law wanted to snap of Ryan's homecoming. I'd say that the time it took to get the baby from the car to the house was roughly double the life span of the average parakeet. Ryan's trip home had now taken up almost two and a half hours!

The baby, still ensconced in his car seat, ultimately made his way into the house. I was maneuvering him through doorways and around walls, and my wife said to me, "Be careful. Don't drop him." Really. Did she really feel she had to tell me this? I know I'm not the sharpest crayon in the box, but do I actually need to be instructed to not drop an infant? My mind searched for a few smartass remarks to toss back, but then I just let it go. She had been through a lot in the last few days, so I decided to cut her some slack. Plus, I couldn't think of anything good to say.

Somehow we finally reached our destination, the bedroom. This was where we took Ryan out of his car seat and put him down into his bassinet. It was at this point for us— as it will be for you, my friend—that a very tired baby and his exhausted mommy and daddy laid down for a much-needed nap. A very short-lived, much-needed nap.

# Man vs. Beast (Or in This Case, Infant vs. Kitten)

AS ANY PARENT of even a week-old baby could have told us (remember, Ryan was not yet a week old—we had a good excuse for being naïve), we weren't really able to sleep very long. Ryan's hungry belly woke him up. And woke us up. Ryan let us know in no uncertain terms that he was not very happy about the situation. His crying piqued the interest of our up-until-now oblivious cat Oliver, who apparently had only now noticed that there was a baby in the house. Oliver jumped up onto our bed and peered over into the bassinet, then looked at us like,

"Uh, what the hell is that?" So we properly introduced the cat and the baby, and neither of them was overly impressed with the other. Ryan was still insisting on having a breast in his mouth, and the cat was searching for someplace to hide from the squealing noise coming from the bassinet. I think in the back of his little kitty brain, Oliver knew that his day in the sun had passed.

It's interesting how perspectives change once you have a child. Before the baby came along, we doted on our cat, as do a lot of pet owners. Childless couples often have photo albums filled with pictures of their pets from when they were first brought home. They have the best chew toys that money can buy. They hire pet-sitters for when they go out of town. Pets have the ability to persuade full-grown adults to speak baby talk to them. "Who's my little angel? Who wants a snack? Gimme kisses, baby. . . . "

We were no exception. We treated Oliver like a human member of the family. Actually, we treated him better than we treat our other family members. He was, in our minds, the baby. But then you bring your child home, the furry little member of the family quickly gets reduced to a "pet." An "animal." A third-class citizen. It's through no fault of their own, but it's the truth. Soon, the pictures in the photo album of little Pookie, or whatever God-awful moniker you've bestowed upon your animal, are being replaced by those of your kid. And your pets soon lose their identity, going from names like "Sparky" to "the damn dog," as in "the damn dog barked and woke the baby up again" or "the damn dog is humping the baby's leg again." From the penthouse to the doghouse. The food chain is a real bitch, isn't it, Pookie?

# Father Knows Breast

WHEN MY WIFE HAD DECIDED she wanted to breast-feed months earlier, I supported it. Countless studies show that this method of feeding a baby is much healthier. Research has found that breast-fed babies have higher IQs than their formula-fed peers. Also, breast-fed babies have fewer ear infections and suffer fewer bouts with diarrhea. Plus, breast-feeding helps the mother lose most of the weight that was gained during pregnancy. (However, this doesn't apply to the now fat-ass dads who inevitably pack on almost as much weight during that time, and I should know.) Overall, breast-feeding sounded like the right thing to do. I was proud of my wife for making the decision to do this, and I applauded her for it just as you should do if you are placed in a similar situation. Remember our motto? Nod, smile, and say "OK."

The bad thing about breast-feeding is that the man's role in this whole thing is very small. Once again, I was back to feeling useless, just as I had during the first part of the pregnancy. The newborn phase is kind of a rip-off for us dads. The mothers get to bond with the baby, spending quality time with them while providing them with the sustenance the child needs for survival. We can only sit on the sidelines with our "just-for-show" nipples and watch.

Of course, you could encourage your wife to pump breast milk into a bottle so that you can be the one to feed your new child. She'll think you're tremendously helpful and selfless until someone clues her (if she doesn't know already!) to the fact that switching to a bottle this early on may cause nipple confusion. That's right, nipple confusion. Did you ever think you'd hear me say that or that you yourself would ever read it? Most red-blooded males know what nipples are . . . how could anybody be confused by them, right?

Well, defense is the best offense, so listen up and try to understand what you're up against here. Babies are born knowing how to suckle, but they use different techniques to get milk from a breast and a bottle. Generally, breast-feeding requires more forceful sucking motions and greater muscle coordination than bottle-feeding. Babies use forty facial muscles to breast-feed effectively and only four to suck on a bottle. If you give bottle nipples (or even pacifiers) to your newborn, the baby can actually forget how to nurse properly. This confusion can lead to diminished or discontinued nursing. Nipple confusion is generally not a problem after the first few weeks of life, once your baby is nursing well. I guess it's kind of like taking the "Pepsi Challenge." If you are so sure you're a Pepsi drinker and it turns out that you enjoyed a Coke that someone gave you without your knowledge . . . well, that would just blow you away.

So you may be asking yourself, "If the mother does the breast-feeding, what do I get to do?" We get the oh-so-fun task of changing the poopy diapers. For at least the first few weeks of parenthood, fathers get the shit end of the stick, if you'll pardon the pun. More often than not, my wife would finish feeding our son and then hand him off to me for the diaper-changing ritual. To be honest, I'm not sure I saw my son's face for the first month of his life. It was either planted up against my wife's breast or was hidden behind his legs, which were straight up in the air as I was wiping his little baby butt.

# I'm So Tired,
# I Haven't Slept a Wink . . .

I HAD NEVER BEFORE REALIZED the effects on a human body that sleep deprivation can have. It's amazing. Our son didn't sleep through the night for the first month and a half. So in that time, neither Julie nor I got any real rest at all. During the first few weeks of our baby's life, we slept so little that I was hallucinating. I thought I saw a beer bottle go walking by me one day. I also could have sworn that I could hear myself blink one night.

Then there was the constant incoherent babbling to coworkers and friends, and then I would just cry for absolutely no reason. I thought my brain was dying. Sleeping is an underappreciated privilege of which I now understand the value. Too bad rest isn't something you can stockpile, or I would have slept in more often in our pre-baby days.

When Ryan would wake up at all hours, we took turns rocking him, walking up and down the halls with him, singing to him, or just talking to him. I know on more than one occasion I tried actually reasoning with my son. Have you ever tried to strike a deal with a three-week-old baby? It doesn't work. They don't adhere to the agreement. I promised my son on many a night that if he would just sleep for six or seven hours straight, I would run out the very next day and buy him a Mustang. We even shook on it. But what happened three hours later? "Waah!" Hey, it's his loss. No high-powered sports cars for him. He broke the contract.

More often than not, when he woke up in the middle of the night, Ryan wanted to be fed. So this meant that Julie had to get out of bed, whip out a tit and let him go at it. Again, not being able to help her with this, I felt guilty. So I would often get up with her, stumble into his room, stub a toe or two, and just sit on the floor next to the rocking chair while she fed him. She kept telling me to go to bed, but I just couldn't do it. I thought that if she had to go through this, by God so would I. What a sucker. Love for a wife and child knows no bounds. Plus, I'm not very logical at three in the morning.

So I sat there on the cold floor and watched Ryan bury his face into an area where I hadn't been allowed in quite some time. Then as soon as he was done feeding, I would offer to burp and rock him. So what did she do? She hopped her happy ass back into bed! Now I'm sitting here burping the baby, who is looking at me like, "Dude, I'm wide open. Wanna play Texas Hold 'Em or something?" So we'd stay up and watch television, which really blows at three in the morning, by the way. There is absolutely nothing on at this time of the night. Even if you have a satellite dish with 500 channels or whatever, you will have seen everything there is to see by week two of this little ordeal. I bet I watched Leif Garrett's "Behind the Music" on VH-1 at least three dozen times. His life is like a car crash. I know it's awful, but I can't turn away for some reason. . . .

Pretty soon, as you'll see, the exhaustion gives way to irritability. You and your wife will start bickering at each other in ways that you could never imagine, and for reasons that are, well, unreasonable. You will both snap at each other out of frustration and fatigue. Even the slightest question will be enough to set you off. "Honey, what time is it?" "Time? I'll tell you what time it is. It's time for you to get your damn watch fixed. What am I, Big Ben? There's a clock six feet away from you, for crying out loud!"

Yes, indeed. The moodiness you experience through lack of sleep is truly an amazing thing. You begin to think that your baby is some sort of mad scientist, placed here to perform an experiment on sleep deprivation, and you and your wife are his lab rats.

When you're feeling your worst, there is one thing that can help you feel better. If you're smart, you've used this quiet meditation before. Take the crankiness you're feeling and multiply it by ten. This will give you a rough idea of what your wife is going through, thanks to postpartum mood swings, sometimes called the "baby blues." It's been said that 60 to 80 percent of all new mothers experience this. Their hormones are going ape-shit and abruptly decreasing in levels immediately after childbirth. This, coupled with the lack of sleep, causes the postpartum mother to be extraordinarily cranky. These same hormones may cause her to slip into a clinical form of postpartum depression or PPD. The signs of PPD include uncontrollable weepiness, change in appetite, panic attacks, and even suicidal thoughts. Experts have yet to come up with a precise explanation, but they agree that PPD is caused by a combination of hormonal, biochemical, environmental, psychological, and genetic factors. Also—outside of all the clinical jargon—the emotional high of giving birth and being one with nature and the "circle of life" and all that bullshit disappears quickly and is replaced by the many new responsibilities and all the crap that comes with parenthood. Taking care of a newborn can be difficult and at times maddening, especially for a first-time mom. So just be on the lookout for these signs, and perhaps talk to your wife's doctor if you really become concerned. In the meantime, stay the hell out of her way.

Something else you may want to consider at this point is—and I cannot stress this enough—do not attempt a lighthearted practical joke on your wife at this time. Take it from me. Just don't do it. I'm going to tell you what I did once *only* if you promise never to do it to her. And if you *do* decide to do this, don't blame me for the results. I am not liable for what happens to you if you try this at home.

When Ryan was about a week and a half old, I was walking him around the house trying to console him. He was crying for what was, as far as I could tell, no good damn reason. So I was pacing the halls with him as Julie was in the kitchen washing the dishes. One thing we had already learned that would calm him down was a *Sesame Street* Talking Ernie doll. Note: This doll was roughly the same size as our baby at this time. We'd make the doll talk, the kid would calm down, and our will to live would begin to return, if only for a moment. So here's what I—a prankster extraordinaire—did:

I stopped pacing for the moment, I sat Ryan (who was, it should be noted, still crying) down on the couch, wrapped the Ernie doll up in a blanket and walked into the kitchen holding it. I kept on talking and pretending to console the baby, saying things like, "Shh. You're OK. Come on. Shh. . . ." Julie wasn't paying much attention at this time. All she knew was the baby was crying and it appeared that we were both coming into the kitchen to see her.

Well, instead of handing her the baby, I pretended to trip, said, "Whoa!" and threw Ernie across the kitchen! She let out a blood-curdling scream, because as far as she could tell, her infant son was airborne and about to smash his little nose into the linoleum! Of course, she quickly realized that something was amiss, because I was doubled over on the floor laughing, and her *real* son was still in the living room. She smacked me a few times and called me a bastard.

In my defense, I admit that at just about the exact moment when I let go of Ernie, I thought to myself, *Oops. This was probably a bad idea.* I mean, I had a sense that this hormonal woman was going to freak out. But by the time my mind processed all of this, I had already pretended to toss her first-born across the room. Hey, we needed a tension breaker. It simply had to be done. And after she stopped kicking and smacking me, she laughed about it. Not as much as I did, but she laughed. Plus, the way I look at it, that's what she gets for always telling me, "Dada, be careful. Don't drop him."

# Dada

AMAZINGLY SOON AFTER your child is born, your given name will start to disappear from use. In my case, it was replaced by "Dada." "Dada, will you get a diaper and some wipes?" "Dada, someone's getting tired." When it happens the first time, you think it's cute. It's almost like a new pet name or something, replacing past favorites like "Honey" or "Sweetheart." (Remember, I refuse to talk about sex when I know my mother will read this book. Be content with Honey and Sweetheart here; insert your own pet names if you like.) Soon it just becomes commonplace, and you don't even really notice that she has totally discarded your true name and replaced it with this moniker.

Then, after a while, you catch yourself referring to yourself in the third person, using the new nickname when you're talking to your baby. "Dada's got you. Shh. It's OK. Dada's here." Before long, you've completely abandoned the name you were given at birth and you've taken on a new handle. The artist formerly known as you is now the human pooper scooper currently known as Dada.

Given the fact that I had been handed this new name, I decided to use it to my advantage. I was bound and determined to have my son's first word be "Dada." So I repeated it to him at least 200 times a day, just to get it stuck in his head. It's kind of like hearing a song with a catchy phrase that remains permanently imbedded in your brain after you listen to it. How many nights have you lain in bed wanting to hang yourself because the ending of "Hey Jude" was playing over and over in your head, keeping you from going to sleep? Every time you'd start to drift off and thought you had the problem licked, suddenly it was as if someone had put a quarter in the jukebox of your mind and played the damn thing over again: Just as you're about to lose consciousness, you hear "Na, na, na, na, na, na, na . . . na, na, na, na, Hey Jude!" *Dammit!*

See, this is the logic I was using with my baby boy. If I could get the word "Dada" stuck in his head, he would be forced to use it as his first word, if for no other reason than to get it out of his head.

But my wife was soon wise to my game, and she started doing the same thing to the baby. Only she was trying to get him to say "Mama." Let the games begin. I soon learned that it was not beneath Julie to play dirty. While she and I were using similar tactics, she had a slightly better strategy. She one-upped me, because whereas I would say, "Dada is getting you a bottle, Ryan," she would say, "Mama is getting you a bottle, isn't Mama?" Sneaky bitch. She was getting upwards of 50 percent more "Mamas" in with techniques of that sort. Damn, she was good. Somehow that had to be considered cheating, but since we hadn't established any rules for this contest, I had no case.

Soon we were both walking around trying to outdo the other and talking about ourselves in the third person all day long. And what was the baby doing? He was simply giving us that blank stare that only a two-month-old child (or a supermodel) could do. He had no interest in playing this game. He was just amused by what great lengths his parents would go to just to win his approval. He didn't say his first word until a few months later. When he eventually said his first word, it was . . . Mama. I've yet to make my concession speech. I demand a recount.

# The Partnership

HOW ANYTHING SO LITTLE can captivate me and occupy my every thought, I'll never know. But that's exactly what my son did, and continues to do. I have always been fascinated by his every move. When he was just weeks old, he would just lie on the floor, stare up at the ceiling and move each finger and toe individually, very slowly and decisively. It was like he was counting to twenty over and over again, and doing so in slow motion. He could also grip almost any object using only his toes. This mesmerized me. He could grab my fingers, my shirt, the cat's tail, a Nerf ball, and anything else his foot came into contact with. I think that if I had taken him outside, he could have grasped a tree limb using only his toes and he would have been able to hang upside down like a bat. I asked, but Julie wouldn't let me try. If I have one complaint about my wife, it's that she's never been overly adventurous when it comes to her son.

Other things fascinated me about our son as well. Babies will smile at absolutely nothing, and I gotta say, I found this very interesting. My son would be staring off into space and just grinning a beautifully toothless smile. But I could never figure out what he was smiling at. I would look in the same general direction as he, but I only saw the wall. This is what fascinated me. Was he like the kid in *The Sixth Sense*? I almost expected him to look over at me and whisper, "I see dead people." But the most I ever got out of him was "Mama." Then he would go back to gawking at absolutely nothing. He would basically look intently at the wall or the carpeting or whatever and just be as giddy as a little drunken monkey. How can this be entertaining? What the heck is this kid smiling at? The carpeting is not that funny. I tried staring at it just to see what he found so enjoyable about it. And while I found it slightly more amusing than most prime-time sitcoms, the carpeting simply could not hold my attention for very long. But he loved it for some reason. We had literally hundreds of dollars worth of baby toys that squeaked, squealed, beeped, lit up, played music, went "choo-choo" and sang the ABCs over and over, yet he was happier gazing into the pseudo-shag carpeting in our living room.

Don't you wish you could be so effortlessly amused? Of course, who is more easily entertained—the boy who is staring and smiling at the carpet or the grown man who is laughing at the boy who is staring and smiling at the carpet? So this fascinated me as well. I thought to myself, *As soon as he can talk, I'm going to ask him what was so damn funny. I hope he doesn't forget by then.*

I also liked doing something as simple as bottle-feeding him. It was such a peaceful and relaxing thing to do. And I think I had a pretty good feeding technique as well. I would lay him on a pillow, slightly elevated with his head down at my knees and his feet resting on my stomach. I would hold the bottle in one hand, freeing up my other hand so I could either use the remote control or drink my beer. (Hey, he has *his* bottle, and I have *mine*, OK?) But I just used to love watching him drink from his bottle. I loved watching his face muscles (all four of them) move around in order to work at suckling. I loved when he would stop in middrink, look at me and smile for really no other reason than to say, "Hey. How ya doin'?" I also loved how he would stop drinking every so often, catch his breath and start drinking again. It reminded me of when I was a kid. You know how you would come running into the house on a hot summer day, grab a glass of Kool-Aid and guzzle it down until you completely ran out of breath? Then when you were just shy of passing out, you stop drinking, pant for a few seconds, and chug the rest of the sugar-laced drink? Well, babies do something similar to that. They will stop for a second, huff and puff, then start all over again.

But I really liked when, during the feeding session, Ryan would just grab my finger in his fist and hang on for dear life. What I found interesting about this is the fact that babies have an amazingly strong grip. At times, I couldn't have pried his hand off of my finger with a tire iron. But the first time he ever held onto my finger like that was a pretty neat moment. I realized that he was holding his daddy's hand, and it made me look forward to when he would be doing this over the next few years—before crossing the street, strolling through the park on our way to the playground, or walking up to see Santa. To me, this is what it was all about. Sometimes, while he would be holding my finger, I'd say something like, "We're going to take a nice long nap today, right?" And since he was holding my finger, we'd shake on it and make it an official deal. We had entered into the daddy/son partnership. After we would shake on whatever particular agreement we had made, we would celebrate by both drinking from our favorite bottles.

# I Am the Funniest Man Alive

ONE OTHER THING that I absolutely loved about early parenthood was baby laughter. There is no sound in the world quite as wonderful and heartwarming as the laughter of a baby. The very thought of it gets me high as a kite. I wish I could contain baby laughs in a jar and sell them for $5 a six-pack. It would fly off of the shelves and probably put the major beer breweries out of business. It is an intoxicating feeling that makes you smile, no matter what kind of crappy day you've had up until that point. Ryan's very first laugh was at something I did. This was such a cool feeling.

The first time I made my son laugh, I thought I was the funniest man in the country. I mean, no one had ever made this person laugh before that very moment in time. So that will be my legacy, I guess. I mean sure, I never walked on the moon. I never found a cure for cancer. I never did anything for the greater good of mankind. But by golly, I made my son laugh for the first time. And heaven knows I tried hard to do so.

For the first month or two of his life, I kept trying to make him laugh or smile, with little or no result. He would occasionally give us a little grin. But that was usually due to the fact that he was gassy or about ready to spit up all over my shirt (that I had just changed from the last puking incident). I went to great lengths to force a smile out of this kid. I would jump around, make funny faces, sing silly songs, fall down, hit myself with various toys in the toy box . . . all for nothing. He would blankly stare at me as if to say, "Is that all ya got? Well, leave your résumé with the receptionist. We'll call you. OK, who's next? Mommy, you're up!" But after all of the crazy antics that my wife and I employed to try to make this kid laugh, the one thing that would get him every time was the ceiling fan.

Babies absolutely love ceiling fans for some reason. I can't explain it, but it's true. My wife has said for a long time now that our son's best friend is the fan in our bedroom. When he was really small, he would just lie on his back and grin at that damn fan for hours and be content. It's like baby television or something. And when I asked other parents about this phenomenon, I found that their children would do the same thing. But when I would try to make him smile, I wouldn't get squat. What exactly does the fan have that I don't, other than five blades that swirl around, and four lights with one bulb constantly blown out?

Finally, when he was about two and a half months, I did it. I cracked the code. I said or did something that made my son laugh, although I still cannot figure out what it was. I think I was simply leaning over to give him a kiss good-bye as I headed for the office, said his name, and he cackled like a drunken frat guy listening to a Monty Python record. So I said his name again. More laughter. We must have done this for fifteen minutes straight before he finally got tired of the game. And I was the happiest person in the world. I had made him laugh so hard that tears were running down his cheeks. Finally, my hard work had paid off big time. So we amended our daddy/son partnership with the addition of the following statement: I will continue to feed, clothe, and care for him as long as he promises to laugh for me at least once a day. We shook on it and then I left for work, beaming with pride that I was indeed the funniest daddy in the immediate vicinity.

# What, Me Worry?

**ANYONE WHO KNOWS ME** will tell you that I am a worrier. I fret about things that are well beyond my control. I've never been hurting for things to agonize over. What can I say? It's a talent. Some people can juggle. Some are athletic. Some can play any musical instrument you plop down in front of them. I have the ability to worry about most anything, be it money, my health or the health of a family member or friend, war, school, work, relationship problems, whether or not I remembered to put the trash can out on trash day, plane crashes, car crashes, getting to the required word count needed for this damn book to satisfy my editor . . . you name it, I can lose sleep over it. That is the way I've always been, and I don't see that changing anytime soon. But now that we had a baby, I found that my concerns had only just begun. There were literally hundreds and perhaps thousands of things to worry about now that we had a child. These things range from ridiculous to serious. From the moment you bring the baby home, you begin to stress over things like:

What if I burp him too hard and I snap his spine, causing him to spend his life in a baby-sized wheelchair?

What if I don't burp him hard enough, and no gas escapes, which will cause him to eventually explode?

What if I drop him?

What if I fall asleep while feeding him and I drool into his nostrils and drown him?

What if I don't drool while sleeping, but I fall over on top of him and crush him like a grape?

What if his clothes are too tight?

What if they're too loose?

What if his bath water is too hot or too cold?

What if I leave him in the bath water too long and his skin wrinkles up to the point where it won't ever straighten itself out?

What if I pick him up after his too hot/cold bath, and he's so slippery that he slides right out of my hands and lands in the toilet next to the bathtub?

What if the cat finally decides he has had enough of this screaming kid, so he takes the baby's breath away, like I saw in that movie?

What if the formula in the bottle is too hot? Or too cold?

What if he drops his pacifier in cat shit, and I don't realize it so I give it to him and he catches some kind of weird cat shit disease?

Pranks aside, what if when I'm pacing the hallway in the middle of the night while holding him, I trip on a toy and smack his little head into the wall, injuring his soft spot, making him a vegetable?

What if we find that he is a freak who is allergic to anything hypoallergenic?

What if I'm holding him and I start laughing so hard at something that I inadvertently shake him like a British nanny?

What if, in a state of grogginess, I accidentally give him a bottle of Coke and I drink his formula?

What if I forget and leave him in the car when I go to the mall?

Crazy, you say? Maybe so, but it doesn't get any better the older they get. You still have other things to concern yourself with, well after the baby has gone from infant to toddler to preschooler to school age and beyond. I'm sure that although I am in my thirties, my father still worries about me. And I know that if the stress doesn't kill me before my son reaches adulthood, I'll always worry about him no matter where he goes or what he does in life.

I don't think it ever ends. You always have to have this nervousness in the back of your mind about things such as:

What if he trips and falls and breaks his arm?

What if he falls off of his tricycle and knocks out his teeth?

What if he chases a ball out into the street and gets hit by a car?

What if he tries to feed a Doritos chip to a squirrel and it bites him, so he has to get a rabies shot?

What if, even after repeated warnings, he takes candy from a stranger?

What if he falls behind in math, and comes to me for help when I can't even count to twenty-one without removing both shoes and my pants?

What if he gets bullied at school?

What if he *is* the bully at school?

What if he borrows a book from the library and forgets to take it back, and over time the interest and penalties add up to so much money that the library police come and take my house?

What if he drinks?

What if he does drugs?

What if he gets someone pregnant?

What kind of psychological damage will be done if he doesn't get a date to the prom and ends up going with his mother?

What if he ends up being one of those kids who snaps under the pressure of school work and his part-time job at Arby's and ends up climbing to the top of a bell tower and "offing" a bunch of college students?

What if, on his wedding day, he leaves his bride at the altar and runs away with the maid of honor?

Or the best man?

Or what if he just grows up to become a really wonderful, happy, and well-adjusted man who doesn't need me to worry about him anymore? Maybe that's what I'm most worried about. . . .

# Don't Cry Over Sour Milk

IF YOU ASKED ME TO DESCRIBE early parenthood in a single word, I would have to say that the most fitting word would be "Yuck." Things are very messy at this first stage of the game. From the very beginning, you have the actual birth itself, which is full of blood and other assorted bodily fluids, cords being cut, gross stuff being suctioned out of the baby's nose and mouth, as well as other various hideous things that you'll just have to witness for yourself.

Then you have spit-up. You will find that babies spit up quite frequently during their first few months. They launch this white and cheesy disgusting liquid from their mouths about twenty times a day. After a while you'll start to question whether or not this child is actually getting anything down to their stomach all day long, since they spit up so much. For your information (not that information makes spit up any less gross), the reason they do this is either because they swallow air during feedings or because they've eaten too much. The worst part is that you never know when it's coming or how much they'll spew out. They will typically either trickle one or two mouthfuls of milk down their chin, which you can just wipe up before going on about your business; *or* they seemingly explode onto your freshly washed favorite shirt just as you're heading off (late) to work, and you get to walk around all day smelling like you took a shower in curdled milk. One trick to reducing the amount of chunky burps is this: You can help your baby expel any swallowed air and reduce the amount he spits up by burping him about every three to five minutes during feedings. But there's a catch: Don't interrupt him midswallow; instead, just wait for his natural pauses. And don't bounce the baby up and down on your knee or spin them around and around for at least a half hour after they've eaten (trust me on this, I speak from experience).

The Yuck factor doesn't end here. Aside from the spit-up and the obvious poopy diapers, you'll also likely get the added bonus of dealing with drool. Drool is a sticky and translucent substance that drips copiously from your child's mouth, indiscriminately soaking all material within a thirty-foot radius. Your shirt, your pants, the baby's clothing, the couch, the carpet, the cat's back. . . . Anything that comes into the drool's path is fair game. You can see the drool start to form on your baby's bottom lip, and if you are able to move fast enough, you might be able to stop it from continuing its march out of the mouth. But if you have to walk over to where the burp cloths are, you'll be too late. The drool will have gone from a tear-drop-sized formation inside the baby's lip to one long strand of disgustingness that is now pooling on your couch. It's inevitable. Oh well. I mean, you didn't like that old furniture anyway, did you?

# "This'll Hurt Me More Than It'll Hurt You"

AS FAR BACK AS I CAN REMEMBER, I always wanted to be a gangster—no, wait, that's the opening narrative line from *Goodfellas*; my fault. What I meant to say is, as far back as I can remember, I always hated going to the doctor. From the time I was old enough to recollect the previous visit, I dreaded going in for the next appointment. Still, to this day I detest everything that is involved with going to the doctor's office. Let's start with the waiting room. In my experience, the waiting room always seemed to have an overly wrought floral wallpaper, peeling off in two of the four corners of the room. Poorly drawn pictures of canvasback ducks and paintings of mountain ranges framed in cheap, ugly pseudo-wood were hanging on the walls. Hey, this was Tennessee, but I'm willing to bet that you could replace canvasback ducks with your own regional fauna and I've described your doctor's office, too. Even as a child, I always wondered who painted these horrid pictures. Was it the doctor's wife? Did Mrs. Doctor sit around the house all day, watch reruns of Bob Ross on PBS, and try to emulate his works of art? Or did someone actually go out and buy these dreadful things?

To save your own sanity and divert your attention from these aesthetic nightmares, you, like me, probably turned to the magazines that were all stacked up on the table next to you. Depending on what periodicals the doctor subscribed to, you could almost always find at least one old *Life* magazine featuring the latest interview with Nikita Khrushchev. Or you might have flipped through a *People* magazine featuring an article on how breakdancing is becoming all the rage among our kids today. Nothing was ever current. It was maddening, right? But no matter if this was a pediatrician's office, a dentist's office, or even your grandfather's proctologist's waiting room, you could always be certain that you'd find *Highlights* magazine to occupy your time. For the few of you not familiar with *Highlights*, this was a magazine for kids that featured games, stories, and activities that would bore you to the point where you welcomed finally going into one of the inner rooms for a booster shot, because even though you were about to get stuck in the ass with a needle, it would be much less painful than having to do even one more brain teaser or a connect-the-dot puzzle. "Oh, gee. I connected all the dots and made another damn star. Wheeeeee!"

Another thing that always bothered me about going to a doctor's office (and this still applies today) was wondering about all the other people sitting in the waiting room. Why were they there? Most of them looked healthy enough. So why were they coming in to see the doctor? Was this just for a checkup? Or did they have some sort of airborne disease that they were spreading to me and everyone else in the room by simply being there? I wanted to hold my breath for the entire duration of my wait.

Then, of course, after you actually do hear your name called by the nurse, you walk into the little inner room, which is just a smaller version of the waiting area with more damn ducks! (K-Mart must have had a sale on duck pictures or something.) When the nurse leaves the room, she says, "The doctor will be right in to see you." Well, if you've been to a doctor's office more than twice in your life, you know that this statement is absolute crap. The doctor won't really be "right in." The doctor is in the can. He's smoking a cigarette and flipping through a Pier 1 Imports catalog to see what he's going to buy with your money. So you wait. And while you wait, you stare at a glass jar filled with tongue depressors, the box of used needles hanging on the wall . . . and you quietly wonder why his bottle of liquid hand soap on the sink is still full. Hasn't he washed his hands today? Clearly, you're not his first appointment for the day. So why is that damn bottle still overflowing with soap? Just about this time, the doctor walks in. He looks at you, says hi, checks your chart, sticks a needle in your arm, hands you your chart, tells you to call if you need anything, and sends you to the front desk in order to fork over the better part of your life savings. And you leave sore, poor, and unfulfilled.

But I digress. As unpleasant as that experience was, it is ten times as bad the first time you take your baby to the doctor for his or her first round of shots. Because going into this, you *know* what is about to happen. Your baby is just sitting in the car seat, smiling and kicking and playing with an old straw from McDonald's that you left in the back seat about six months ago. Exactly how the child reached it and got hold of it, you'll never know. And frankly, that's the least of your worries at this point. The poor kid is completely unaware of what is about to happen, and you feel a tremendous sense of dread and guilt in knowing that he'll be blindsided and will, perhaps, hold you accountable for the ambush. You keep repeating over and over, "It'll be OK. Don't worry." But who exactly are you reassuring here? You or the baby?

Julie and I decided that we were both going to take our son in for his first round of shots. Neither one of us wanted to be the sole bad guy in this situation. Personally, I tried everything to rig it so that Julie would be the bad guy of record. I considered concocting a single *big* excuse to give her that encompassed every reason I could come up with, just so I'd have all the bases covered. "Honey, I'd like to go with you, but I've got a busy day here at work. And I was already late, due to the fact that on the way in, the car broke down, so I had to push it six blocks, and after heaving it uphill the entire way, I had a stroke. And although I'm feeling a little better after the stroke incident, I think I'm getting a cold, which means that if I went with you I could make the other children in the waiting room sick." But in the end I had to bite the bullet, face the music, buckle down, round up my clichés, and join her in taking our baby to his first doctor's appointment.

When we walked in the door, my wife and the baby went over and sat in the waiting area. I walked up to the little window and signed him in for his very first appointment.

There, the very nice lady at the front desk asked me for Ryan's insurance card and Social Security card. As I was pulling these out, something struck me as being somewhat humorous. On the back of Ryan's social security card, it says that for security precautions and safety concerns, you should sign your card in ink immediately upon receiving it. Now, Ryan was six weeks old when his Social Security card came to us in the mail. The thought of him signing his Social Security card, holding an ink pen in his tiny little newborn fingers was enough to make me chuckle out loud. The lady at the desk just kind of looked at me. I tried explaining to her what I found so funny, but I don't think I told the story very well. She smiled politely and promptly closed the window. I guess something got lost in the translation. . . .

I joined Julie and Ryan over in the waiting area. As is tradition, we sat in the waiting area for about thirty minutes past our appointment time. Such a wait is tedious enough if you are waiting by yourself under normal circumstances. But to be left in a holding pattern for such a long time with an impatient infant slated for his first routine medical ordeal is enough to cause an ordinary man to have an ulcer. We spent a great deal of time trying to find something to amuse him. "Look, Ryan. See that picture on the wall? That's called a duck!" (Damn you, K-Mart!) After spending twenty minutes pacing around with Ryan and looking at other kids while wondering what disgusting illnesses they had, our son's name was finally called. Julie and I walked down the hall toward the room where Ryan would get his first shot. She and I were nervous wrecks, but our son was still blissfully ignorant as to what was about to occur. The walk from the waiting room to the examination room, although only about a twenty foot distance, seemed to take forever.

When we entered the examination room, the nurse told us to undress our son completely, with the exception of his diaper. As we were stripping him down, a look of concern came over his face. We do not normally undress him in public, so he clearly felt that something was amiss. They weighed him on what appeared to be a glorified grocer's scale, and then they measured his head. At first, I wasn't sure what the purpose of measuring his head was. I thought perhaps they were fitting him for a little hat or something. Then it was explained to me that they were just checking his head circumference to make sure he was growing at a normal rate. Then he was returned to the exam room. After waiting another twenty minutes or so, we finally saw the doctor.

Our son's doctor, a very sweet and knowledgeable woman named Dr. Morgan, entered the room and kind of gave us the skinny on what was about to go down. Let me do the same for you. During these first checkups, doctors typically will weigh and measure your baby to make sure they are growing at a healthy rate and will generally list these numbers on a growth chart. The growth chart is a tool that your baby's doctor will use to keep track of your child's physical growth. Think report card here. At each checkup, the doctor will measure the baby's length, weight, and head circumference, and then compare those figures on a chart of national averages for children of the same age and sex as your baby. Damn, another test. In the end, the doctor comes up with the percentile your child falls into. For instance, if your doctor tells you that your four-month-old is in the 80th percentile for height, that means 80 percent of the four-month-old children in the country are smaller and 20 percent are taller.

These percentages always worry me. If my son is in the 40th percentile in height (which he was), then does this mean that 60 percent of all people will be taller than him when he grows up? Will my son be traveling with a touring freak show as the world's shortest baby? Of course, Dr. Morgan had my number; she went on to explain that although he was in the 40th percentile, this was perfectly "normal" (there's that damn word yet again).

The doctor checked our son's hearing and vision, looked in his eyes and mouth, gave his whole body a full once-over, and proclaimed him to be fine and dandy. Then she addressed any questions we had and eased our first-time-parent minds. And just as we were breathing a sigh of relief, the needle came into play. Ryan was about to experience real pain for the first time, and I was not looking forward to it.

He had to get immunized for hepatitis B, pneumococcus, polio, and Hib (this is the Haemophilus influenzae type b bacteria, which can cause severe swelling in the throat that makes it hard to breathe, a serious form of pneumonia, and a disease called bacterial meningitis . . . and the doctor was planning to give Ryan a piece of this?!?!). But that wasn't all. He also had to get a DTP vaccine, which protects against diphtheria, tetanus, and pertussis. All in all, he was about to get four needles jabbed directly into his chubby little infant thighs. I wondered if getting so much deathly stuff on the same day might put him at greater risk of actually getting one of these creeping crud diseases. Yet again, Doc Morgan anticipated my concerns (gee, it's as though she'd heard all this before!) and assured us that the shots had been tested and tested and tested together and separately. Ryan would be better protected with the shots than without them.

The doctor had my wife and I place poor, unsuspecting—although now slightly irritated—Ryan flat on his back on the table with his legs dangling over the edge. Dr. Morgan kind of leaned her body weight against him, wedging his lower legs between the table and her lower torso. She instructed me to hold his arms down so he wouldn't thrash around. By now, he was pissed. He may not know why, but even an infant realizes that someone restraining all of your limbs against your will is not a good thing. Then the doctor administered the shots, and I cannot even describe to you the horror of this situation. You constantly are protecting your child from getting hurt. You keep them from falling. You feed them so they don't experience hunger pains. You try to make sure that they remain out of harm's way at any cost. You do everything in your power to avoid anything bad happening to your child. And now you are not only helping the doctor mete out pain by poking needles into your child's leg but you are also paying for this service. Your baby will look at you with tears streaming down their cheeks, and you just know they're thinking, "How can you let this happen to me? You're supposed to be shielding me from strangers trying to hurt me, not helping them! And let go of my arms, you traitor!" It's a helpless feeling that you just cannot make go away. I'm sure that sometime in your life you've heard, "This is going to hurt me much more than it'll hurt you." Well, this was the first time that those words ever rang true for me. The pain that our son felt was over in a matter of seconds. We were still feeling the sting of this experience for a long time after.

Once Dr. Morgan had finished torturing our son, she placed little Bugs Bunny bandages on his wounds, and the appointment was over with. We dressed him, put him in his car seat, and went home. By the time we left the parking lot, Ryan was giggling and playing with his now-favorite straw as if nothing had happened. He was completely over the whole situation. Instead of comforting him, I spent the rest of the car ride home consoling his mommy, who was saying things like, "The doctor was mean to him. She hurt my baby." And just as I was about to say something sweet and comforting, she turned on me, saying, "And you held his arms down too hard."

# My Kid Is Better
# Than Your Kid . . .

**WHEN OUT WALKING** with your new family (wife and child, that is), you'll likely recognize the following group dynamic when you come across another couple with their offspring in tow. This is as inevitable—and as natural, by the way—as the mating ritual of the giant panda that was documented so well on Mutual of Omaha's *Wild Kingdom*. First, you'll peer down at the other couple's child resting peacefully in his stroller and you'll hear your wife say something like, "Hi there, Sweetie. What's your name? Aren't you adorable?" Meanwhile, the other couple will be staring down at your little one, with your wife's counterpart cooing at your baby similarly. Usually, at this point you are just standing there with your hands in your pockets, sort of staring at the other guy with a closed-mouth half smile and uttering mundane phrases back and forth like, "What a day, huh?" "Yeah. Unseasonably warm, isn't it?" "Can't wait for spring." "Yeah, I hear that!" Then your wife will bring you into her meaningful conversation with a remark like, "Oh, look at this baby. Isn't he a cutie?"

This is your cue to look down at the youngster in the stroller and dish out compliments on how adorable and attractive this other kid is. Now, in all reality, what you're thinking is how much this thing looks like a cross between Mickey Rooney and a spider monkey. But even without coaching, you'll know you can't come right out and say this. I mean, that's not even an option. And you sure as hell can't run away screaming at the top of your lungs about how butt-ugly this little creature is. "Get that freak away from my baby! The ugly disease might be contagious!" This is considered unacceptable, even in most Third World countries. So instead of speaking the truth, offending the other parents, and mortifying your bride, you fire off a couple of noncommital, pseudocompliments like "Aww" and "Ooo." This will seem to satisfy the other parents, and it will get you off the hook. You won't have had to lie, yet the sounds that you emitted will have made it seem as if you thought this pediatric beast wasn't nearly as hideous as it truly is.

But lest you feel superior, you need to understand that the same thoughts are going through the minds of the other parents regarding your child. It's a rule of nature: No one thinks of their kid as being ugly. Everyone believes that they created the perfect child, and every other kid in the world should bow to show respect for how beautiful their baby is. Of course, if that's the case, then why are there so many ugly people in the world?

Moving right along to the next inevitable exchange: You'll begin to compare and contrast your individual baby-related stories. The pregnancy, how much weight was gained, how much the baby weighed at birth, your baby's sleeping habits, and so on. As a rule, all this is really an attempt to one-up the other couple and make yourself feel better about your or your child's possible inadequacies. It's a defense mechanism that serves to protect you against your own insecurities. And for you ladies out there reading this, I'm sorry, but you are worse about this than men. I'm not trying to sound sexist here. It's just a fact.

When the women start in with comparing their pregnancy stories side by side, I find it best to just step aside and listen, because there is nothing I can contribute here. Neither woman is interested in what the men have to say on this topic. They're just going to listen to each other lie about their individual experience, and then give the same bullshit stories right back at them. If one woman (whom we shall refer to as Woman A) tells the other mother (Woman B) that she gained fifty pounds during pregnancy, then Woman B will say that she only gained twenty, making Woman A appear to be a pig. Or it could go the opposite way. Woman A can tell Woman B that she gained seventy pounds, and it took her almost three months to get back into shape. Then Woman B can say that she gained 300 pounds, blaming it on gestational diabetes, and that it only took her six hours to fit back into her size four jeans. The objective here is for each woman to make the other look like a big heifer, thereby making herself feel better about the king-sized Snickers bar she ate just before this exchange.

But it doesn't stop with comparing pregnancy stories. The childbirth stories are just as bad. Each mother attempts to make the other feel inferior about every aspect of the labor. Either Woman B's labor didn't last as long as Woman A's (making her a stronger person) or the drugs didn't kick in soon enough, forcing Woman B to go experience a natural childbirth and all the pain associated with that. It's embarrassing. They may as well arm wrestle and get it over with.

At this point, they move on to comparing their babies. Both women, who have huge bags under their eyes from not sleeping a wink for the last two months, lie about their baby's sleeping habits.

> WOMAN A: Is your baby sleeping through the night?
> WOMAN B: Yes, ever since the third night.
> WOMAN A: Oh, yeah. Same here. Actually, I believe it was by the second night.

Lies. All lies.

> WOMAN A: Our baby has started rolling over already. It's amazing. How about your son?
> WOMAN B: Uh . . . oh, yeah. Sure. Whenever my son is hungry, he rolls all the way into the kitchen, opens up the fridge and makes a sandwich.

More lies.

Someone is going to Hell for this, I just know it. . . .

After the pissing contest is over (and not a moment too soon), you will finally formally introduce yourselves to this other couple and discuss arrangements for play dates for the children (which will never come to pass). You will once again exchange pleasantries about each other's children and say your good-byes, at which point you are finally free to leave and get on with your day, which will consist of bad-mouthing the other parents and trying to figure out which famous actor their child resembled more closely: Cheetah from the *Tarzan* series or Marcel the monkey from *Friends*.

# The First Post-Baby Date

WITH EVERYTHING THAT HAS CHANGED in your world since your baby was born, you may find that it becomes easy to forget to take the time necessary to maintain your relationship with your wife. You'll find that you spend so much time staring at the little face of your child that you fail to remember the fact that there is another person in the house. Eventually, you will come home from work, walk through the door and your wife will say, "Hi. Who are you?" This is when you know that it is time to hire a baby-sitter, relinquish your roles as Mama and Dada for a few hours, and go out on a real "date" like normal couples have done and will continue to do till the end of time.

This idea sounds simple enough—and if your child is yet unborn, you no doubt can't imagine ever finding this hard, but it is remarkably more difficult than one might imagine. First, you have to find a baby-sitter whom you fully trust to watch your child. Well, in reality this *isn't* the first thing you have to do. The *first* thing you have to do is drum up the will to actually leave your child in the care of another human being. This is extremely hard, because in your heart of hearts you think that if you walk out the front door and leave your child, they will simply be unable to survive without you. But then, perhaps after a few drinks and a Xanax, you buckle down and actually hire someone to watch your little treasure. Then, once you finally decide to place your trust in the hands of a competent caregiver and are preparing to leave, you make a list of details that the baby-sitter should know about. These lists usually start out small, featuring important key points, such as the phone number for the baby's doctor, your cell phone number, and the phone number of the places where you will be for the next couple of hours. Then inexplicably, this tiny list of key points turns into book, which is roughly the thickness of the average medical dictionary. You find that not only have you transcribed the phone numbers of the doctor, your cell phone, the restaurant, and the movie theater; you've also included the phone numbers of any establishment where you *might* happen to be (clubs, ice cream parlors, gas stations, jailhouses, etc.).

Then you'll have to write out detailed instructions on what the baby needs before bedtime. These instructions will include how warm to run the baby's bath (yes, sir, you're going to have a number in mind here, believe me), which toys to use in the bathtub, which bottle to use before you put the baby to bed ("Don't use the bottle with the purple nipple cover on it. That particular bottle makes him gassy at night for some reason"), which books the baby likes to have read before bedtime, and the exact time that the child should be laid down for the night ("8:35 is usually his exact bedtime. If he goes to bed anytime earlier, he'll be up too early the next morning. Any time later than 8:35, and he'll sleep in too late in the morning and won't take a decent nap the next day").

And after you finally leave, rest assured that each of these details will very likely be completely ignored by the baby-sitter, who has now in her head vowed never to baby-sit for your neurotic family ever again.

Assuming you ever actually make it out of the house and aren't suffering from instruction-manual-writer's cramp, you and your wife will no doubt make each other the same promise that all other couples make. You both agree that since this is *your* night, you won't talk about the baby at all. You will just attempt to carry on a conversation like you used to, before you were parents. In order to accomplish this, you start making small talk. You find yourself saying things like:

"Sure is a nice night tonight."

"Yep."

"Are you chilly? You seem a little cold. Want my jacket?"

"No. I'm fine."

(Long pause.)

"Maybe we should call to see if the baby's OK."

"I'll dial."

After you've checked on your baby for the third time and find out that everything is fine, you finally begin to relax. Then the oddest thing happens. You start carrying on a normal, adult conversation with your wife. I remember the exact moment when this happened for me. We were in a restaurant, struggling for non-baby-related items to discuss, and *Bam!* it hit. She made a witty remark, and all of a sudden I started to remember what a funny and intelligent person she was. She was more than just the mother of my little boy. She wasn't merely a milk factory, or someone to hand the baby off to when I'm too tired and have had enough daddy/son bonding. She is an immensely bright person with a great sense of humor. It was as if I had just discovered her all over again. I suddenly remembered what made me fall in love with her in the first place, and I realized just how much I had missed her.

In closing, indulge me and let me give you some parting advice: Remember that it is incredibly important to keep working on your relationship with your child's mother, er, I mean your wife, especially at this stage in the game. You can get caught up in the day-to-day business of being parents and caring for the little person cooing in the next room, and it becomes easy to ignore your own needs or the needs of the other important person in your life. Maintaining a good marriage is imperative not only for your child's sake, but for yours as well. Now if you'll excuse me for a moment, I'm going to go hug my wife.

# Thanks for the Advice. Now Could You Please Shut Up?

HERE'S A UNIVERSAL TRUTH: Everyone has advice on parenthood to give to you, whether you asked for it or not. This advice will come to you from all sorts of people, be it doctors, family members, friends, coworkers, authors of humorous yet ever-so-helpful parenting books, clergy, and even random people you meet on the street. No one lacks an opinion when it comes to how you're raising your baby. When you have a child, suddenly every Tom, Dick, and Harry turns into a Dr. Spock wannabe.

Take it from me, the most irritating advice will come to you from people who do not even have children. It just floors me how these childless know-it-alls try to tell you how to raise and care for your kid, when some of them can't even keep goldfish alive for more than six days (if you're a better man than me, you'll refrain from pointing this out). Case in point: We invited some newlywed friends over for dinner one night, and had a pleasant enough time until the end of the evening when the topic of parenthood came up. They had asked us how well we had adjusted to life with a newborn. At the time, our little boy wasn't sleeping through the night yet, and we mistakenly told them this truth. Instead of keeping their traps shut (they couldn't have been all that interested anyway!), this fully rested, childless couple started doling out advice on how to help our son sleep through the night. "What you ought to do is . . . "

I know they had good intentions, but just because they consider their pets to be their "babies," they are not certified parents. Parenting advice from childless pet owners has as much validity as medical advice from Dr. Seuss. And I've been to this couple's house, by the way. Their houseplants are all either dead or plastic, and they're on their third cat in two years. One fish, two fish, dead and blue fish.

So there.

Even complete strangers have ideas as to how you should raise your baby. We have had people walk up to us in a department store, compliment us on how cute our son is, and then start shelling out advice. "If your baby isn't sleeping through the night you should try feeding him more before bedtime. And I see he's drooling. Chances are he's teething. Better get him a teething ring to chew on!" Again, they mean well. But this is clearly none of their business. They don't know us or our son. And furthermore, they're lucky that I was in a sleep-deprived partial coma at the time, or I might have spouted off something like, "Gee, thanks for the unsolicited advice. Feed him when he's hungry? I never would have thought of that. He also has a load in his diaper. What should I do about that, Mr. Genius?"

The oddest piece of parenting advice I ever received came from an outside source. It was from our exterminator. Here in the southern United States we have all sorts of bugs wandering around, and some of them can get to the approximate size of your average poodle. And since we didn't want our house to be infested with bugs that our son could ride around the house like a pony, we enlisted the services a company I now like to call Dorkin.

On this particular occasion, the "Dorkin" guy came in to provide his monthly services, which consisted of spraying poison all over my walls and floorboards, making the same frivolous comments about how he can't wait until Friday, and then handing me a bill for the pleasure of his company. As he was waiting for me to write out the check, he noticed that my son was completely engrossed in an episode of *Elmo's World*. (I will admit it was a pretty intriguing episode. I remember that "H" was the letter of the day.) As I'm just about to sign the check, the "Dorkin" guy says to me, "You know, you really shouldn't be letting him watch television. It's not good for him." Can you believe it? I had just been chastised by the friggin' "Dorkin" guy!

I don't think I can truly express how irritated I was by this. Here is this guy, this human fly swatter if you will, telling me how I shouldn't be allowing my son to watch this educational television show. I was appalled that a man who kills things for a living was giving me unsolicited parenting advice. And frankly, I'm not going to have my parenting skills judged by anyone who comes into my house smelling like whiskey and cigarettes at 8:30 in the morning and sprays poison on my walls. It's just not going to happen. So I gave this walking can of Raid his payment for services rendered and sent him on his way. Then I changed exterminating companies.

The point of this rant is that you don't need anyone telling you how to be a father. Remember that. It's great guy-to-guy advice. It's the best I've got, actually. And it's the only advice from strangers (me) you need ever take to heart.

The love you will feel for your baby will come as naturally to you as breathing. You'll work out your own deals and you will enter your own daddy/baby partnership. You'll laugh like you never have before. You'll cry more than you'll ever admit to your poker buddies. And you will feel an overwhelming sense of completeness when you look down at your child sleeping in the crib and you realize that you helped create such a perfect little human being.

And if you're like me, perhaps you will, for the first time, understand exactly why you were meant to be "Dada."

One day not too long ago, Ryan and I were outside playing. And even though he was being really well behaved that day, for me it was just one of those bad days. I had just finished what was a particularly bad day at work, and I had wrecked my car the day before in an accident that was my own stupid fault (so *that* was bugging me). I was lying in the grass, staring up at the clouds, and I said to Ryan, who was playing with sidewalk chalk on the driveway nearby, "Buddy, what's it all about? Why do I go through the day-to-day crap? What's the point? Why am I here?" And Ryan, who I thought for sure wasn't even listening to me, looked over, pointed and said, "Dada." I thought that pretty much summed it all up. That is why I'm here. That's my role. And that will be your reason for being as well. "Dada." It is so simple, so right on.

I couldn't have said it any better than he did. I thought, *What a smart boy I have. Ryan is wise beyond his years. A real baby genius, if you will.* At that point, my tiny Einstein accidentally poked himself in the eye with a stick.

Oh, well. Back to "normal" . . .

# SPECIAL THANKS

Special thanks to Marnie Cochran (my editor at Da Capo and personal savior), without whom no one would have been able to read these words. I am humbled by your belief in me and in this book, and I pray to God it lives up to your expectations. I also would like to thank my agent, Frank Weimann, at the Literary Group in New York. Your tireless effort brought me to this point, and I thank you from the bottom of my wallet. And yes, your 15 percent is coming. Be patient.

And a special note to Arthur Marx: I have been a life-long fan of your writings, and your father, Groucho Marx, has been my hero as far back as I can recall. Over the last year or so I have had the honor of calling you a friend and collaborator. It has been a thrill getting to know you and your lovely bride, Lois. You have helped me in ways that I can never repay you, so a simple "Thank you" will have to do for now. Of all the items in my Marx Brothers collection, I cherish our friendship most of all.

Now for the big list. I defy anyone reading this to do so aloud and in one breath: Julie and Ryan for continuing to be my inspiration and reason for being; Ron and Myrna Crider (a.k.a. "Granny and Pops"); Earl and Dianna Akard for allowing me to spend my life with their daughter; the Han family; the Akard family; Brian, Gloria, Lisha, and Jonathon Crider; Chris Carson (my best friend of 21 years and counting); Mick and Gloria Carson; Carrie Carson; Jessica Carson; everyone at Da Capo; the lovely and talented Jenny McCarthy; the incomparable genius of Sid Caesar; Pam Anderson at iUniverse; Darlene Thornburg and family; a certain country diva wannabe for flaking out on a project that freed me up to do this one; Mandi and Patrick Anderson; Richard and Terri Sparks; John, Sara, and Dona-Marie Sparks; Tracy Richman; Elizabeth Fleshman; the Thomas boys; Brittany Carden and family; Tom Rainey and family; Barbie and Keith Butler; Allison Smith; Ben Long; Robert Trowbridge; Stacy Van Cour; Stephanie Van Cour; Greg Pope and family; Deborah Honeycutt; Dennis Morgan; Prentice and Leah Morgan;

Shelley Rogers and family; Laura Roudebush; Hope Garner; Tiffany Tidwell; Echo Caskey; Drew Herche; Nate Helyer; Kevin Vickery; Cory Stewart; Dave and Jennifer Easton; Rebecca Bullion for keeping me sane (or at least as sane as possible); Warren Bullock and family; Sara Dishman; Kerry and Cindy Glisson; Ty Hunt; Holland Nix; Misty Garrity; Lanore Haley and family; Nicole Gill; Misha Joseph; Gabby and Jim Lutton; Polly McCord; Stacey Grosh; Tom Taylor; and whoever invented the Prozac I took daily to help deal with the writing of this book.

# ABOUT THE AUTHOR

Michael Crider is the co-founder, editor, and a staff writer for moviesthatsuck.com and has co-written several short films. He lives in Tennessee with his wife, Julie, and their son, Ryan.

Made in the USA
Lexington, KY
11 November 2013